The 1996 Russian
Presidential Election

Brookings Occasional Papers

The 1996 Russian Presidential Election

Jerry F. Hough
Evelyn Davidheiser
Susan Goodrich Lehmann

BROOKINGS INSTITUTION PRESS
Washington, D.C.

Brookings Occasional Papers

THE BROOKINGS INSTITUTION is a private nonprofit organization devoted to research, education, and publication on important issues of domestic and foreign policy. Its principal purpose is to bring knowledge to bear on the major policy problems facing the American people.

On occasion Brookings authors produce research papers that warrant immediate circulation as contributions to the public debate on current issues of national importance. Because of the circumstances of their production, these Occasional Papers are not subjected to all of the formal review procedures established for the Institution's research publications, and they may be revised at a later date. As in all Brookings publications, the judgments, conclusions, and recommendations presented in the papers are solely those of the authors and should not be attributed to the trustees, officers, or other staff members of the Institution.

Contents

Preface

The process of industrialization seldom features a stable democracy in its early and middle stages. When industrializing countries are democratic, popular pressures almost invariably push their governments to adopt protectionist foreign economic policies and resort to heavy government regulation. With the encouragement of the West, however, the leaders of the former Soviet Union tried to introduce democracy at the same time that they promoted rapid marketization, minimal government regulation, deliberate deindustrialization, and a free-trade foreign economic policy. They hoped that democracy would legitimate the transition and compensate for its painful dislocations.

The 1996 presidential election provides the first crucial test of this experiment. Among the major contenders, the Communist party has promised to redirect economic policy and carry it out at a more evolutionary pace. President Boris Yeltsin has charged that a Communist victory would mean the end of real reform. The outcome of the election both immediately and in the longer run will decide whether the assumptions of the past six years in Moscow have been realistic or naive.

The answers have an importance far beyond the interests of political scientists. Russia remains one of the world's great nuclear powers, and its political development is of critical concern for global peace and security. In addition, the history of the twenty-first century will be dominated by industrialization and urbanization in Asia and Africa. The lessons from the Russian experiment need to be assimilated by these regions and taken into account in the policies of other parts of the world.

This book is designed to provide the background necessary to understand Russia's crucial 1996 presidential election. The authors conducted comprehensive sociological surveys at the time of the December 1993 and December 1995 legislative elections. These surveys permit an exploration of the evolution of

Russian attitudes toward both reform and the major political leaders. The book is based on an analysis of these surveys and a detailed examination of the voting data from the two elections.

Many people have been crucial to the progress of this project. Sociologists in each of seventy Russian regions cooperated in a network to conduct the surveys. Ultimately this book is their book, although they, of course, are not responsible for the analysis or the conclusions. Sergei Tumanov of Moscow University and Mikhail Guboglo of the Institute of Ethnology and Anthropology of the Russian Academy of Sciences drafted the questionnaire and organized the work of the network. Timothy Colton of Harvard University had a key scholarly and organizational role in the 1993 survey. The support of John Steinbruner was vital, and Jim Schneider did heroic work in editing a book that was still being updated ten days before it was published.

The network supporting the Russian surveys was created and financed by the John D. and Catherine T. MacArthur Foundation. Financial support was also provided by the Carnegie Corporation, the Brookings Institution, the United States Information Agency, and especially—and repeatedly—by the Sociology Program of the National Science Foundation.

1

Introduction

The Communist party was the clear winner in the December 1995 Duma election in Russia. It received 22.3 percent of the vote in the party list election as compared with 11.2 percent for the Liberal Democrats of Vladimir Zhirinovsky, 10.1 percent for the government party of Premier Viktor Chernomyrdin, and 6.9 percent for the radical alternative, Yabloko. The Communist faction in the Duma contained 149 deputies, and other factions closely allied with it had 72. This gave the Communist party 49 percent of the seats in the Duma. The 51 deputies of the Liberal Democrats and a dozen or so other oppositional nationalists were expected to support it on most matters.[1]

In itself the left-wing victory in the 1995 Duma election was not especially significant. The Duma has little power, and President Boris Yeltsin further reduced its importance by acting extraconstitutionally. However, the very factors that reduced the significance of the Duma elections have magnified that of the presidential election to be held on June 16, 1996. All politicians have looked upon the Duma election as a trial run for the presidential election, as a testing of public opinion. If the results of the Duma election are replicated in the presidential election, that would, indeed, be highly significant.

A public opinion poll conducted in Russia in March 1996 suggested that in a runoff in a presidential election the Communist candidate, Gennady Zyuganov, would receive 37 percent of the vote and Yeltsin 29 percent, with 34 percent of the people undecided. Those are approximately the figures that would be predicted from the 1995 Duma election results. However, most of the undecided in Russia are not apathetic: they are clearly suspicious of the Communists and hostile toward Yeltsin. If they will face a choice between the two in the runoff, they will select the man they consider the lesser of two evils or at least the lesser of two risks.

The crucial question is whether Zyuganov is like Patrick Buchanan in the U.S. Republican party in 1996—a candidate with a strong base of support but a ceiling of suspicion through which he will not be able to break and obtain a majority position. Or does the gain the Communists made between 1993 and 1995 position them to acquire the absolute majority needed to elect a president, especially given the unpopularity of the other candidate? If the Communists do achieve a majority, and that is the most probable outcome in the election, what are the implications for Russia and for the United States?

These questions are the subject of this book. Since 1992 two of the authors, Jerry Hough and Susan Goodrich Lehmann, have collaborated in conducting major, long-term sociological surveys to study the evolution in political attitudes and social structure in Russia during the transition after the collapse of the Soviet system.

Since 1993 they have worked with Sergei Tumanov, head of the Sociology Center of Moscow University, and Mikhail Guboglo, first deputy director of the Institute of Ethnology and Anthropology of the Russian Academy of Sciences, and a network of sociologists, ethnographers, and political scientists in each of the oblasts (regions) and former autonomous republics of the Russian republic on these projects. The network was established in 1993 by the John D. and Catherine T. MacArthur Foundation, which has provided another grant in 1996 and 1997 for further training and work with it. This group of Russian scholars conducted the 3,900-respondent 1993 election study used here.[2] It also conducted an examination of language assimilation in four former republics of the Soviet Union and two Russian republics,[3] and an examination of religion and ethnicity in four Russian republics.[4]

Hough and Lehmann joined with Evelyn Davidheiser to conduct a national random survey of 3,827 respondents in Russia.[5] At the time of the 1995 election Davidheiser examined in detail the surprising reversal in the regional patterns of voting in the 1990s from what it had been before the 1917 revolution. She also went to Moscow both at the time of the 1993 and 1995 elections to study the campaigns of the left-wing and nationalist parties. The 1995 survey employed the methodology, the Russian polling team, and most of the questions of the 1993 survey. This created the opportunity not only to assess the state of opinion in Russia in 1995 and the sources of support for and opposition to the Communist party but to understand the evolution that has occurred since 1993.

The Centrality of City and Countryside in Russian Politics

In all elections since 1989 the large cities in Russia provided the strongest support for economic reform and democracy and for Boris Yeltsin and his government, while the villages, towns, and smaller cities were the primary base of conservative support.[6] In 1989 Yeltsin received 89.6 percent of the vote in the USSR election in a district that embraced all of Moscow, the largest center of the defense industry and bureaucracy in the country. In 1990 he received a like percentage in the great Urals industrial center of Sverdlovsk (now Ekaterinburg) in the elections for the Russian Congress. In the June 1991 presidential election, his Communist opponent, Nikolai Ryzhkov, did well only in the countryside.

Yeltsin received a particularly high percentage of the vote because of his personal appeal at that time, but the difference in the voting behavior among those living in villages, towns, and large cities has been a general and persistent one. In the 1989 elections to the USSR Congress of People's Deputies and the 1990 election to the Russian Congress of People's Deputies, the size of the largest city in an electoral district had an enormous effect on the type of deputy it was likely to elect (see table 1-1 for the pattern in the 1990 Russian election). The largest cities overwhelmingly elected supporters of radical change; the smaller cities, the towns, and the villages elected more conservative deputies. A similar relationship was found in the 1993 and 1995 Duma elections.[7] When Ralph Clem and Peter Craumer examined county-level data, they found the most rural counties—those with the largest rural populations and those farthest from the oblast capital—were more conservative than those closer to the cities.[8]

Because the northern part of Russia has poor quality land and a short growing season (analogous to northern New England), it is limited in the number of

Table 1-1. Political Orientation of Deputies, by Size of City in Which They Were Elected, RSFSR Territorial Districts, March 1990

Population of largest city in electoral district	Radical deputies	Moderate deputies	Conservative deputies	Total
Less than 25,000	17	29	90	136
25,000–49,999	40	36	91	167
50,000–99,999	51	42	60	153
100,000–199,999	24	19	24	67
200,000–499,999	50	30	34	114
500,000–999,999	52	23	17	92
More than 1,000,000	35	22	13	70
St. Petersburg	27	1	2	30
Moscow	52	5	0	57

Source: Jerry F. Hough, *Democratization and Revolution in the USSR, 1985–1991* (Brookings, forthcoming).

Table 1-2. Attitude toward Communist Party among Total Population and Workers Age 18–59, by Population of Place of Residence, December 1993

Percent

Population of place of residence	Attitude toward Communists			
	Positive	More positive than negative	More negative than positive	Negative
Total population				
Less than 50,000	32	20	10	37
50,000 to 199,999	24	15	7	59
200,000 to 999,999	14	13	18	54
More than 1 million	13	10	13	68
Workers				
Less than 49,999	28	22	10	40
50,000 to 199,999	27	16	4	52
200,000 to 999,999	13	11	16	60
More than 1,000,000	15	8	10	67

Sources: Based on the 1993 poll of Russian respondents. See text. Those without an opinion are excluded.

people it can support in agriculture, and the area has become urbanized. Most rural people live on the more fertile land at more southerly latitudes. Thus the difference in the voting behavior of people living in cities and towns of different size became the basis for one of the most noted cleavages in Russian politics— that between the more radical north and the more conservative south.[9] (The dividing line in political terms is about 55 degrees latitude, with Moscow being located at 55 degrees, 45 minutes.)

The same pattern was found in our 1993 election survey, both for the population as a whole and for selected groups. Since attitudes toward Communists are crucial for the book, we will use the question on that subject in tables 1-2 and 1-3 to show the impact of place of residence on attitudes, but the general point could be replicated with a variety of questions.[10]

As these tables show, the great problem for the Communist party in 1993 was that it had lost the allegiance of the young and the "real proletariat"—the industrial workers in large plants in the major cities. Yet the workers in cities with less than 200,000 people were not nearly as opposed to the party as those in cities with more than 1,000,000.

Table 1-3. Positive Evaluation of the Communist Party, by Age and Population of Place of Residence, December 1993

Percent

Population of place of residence	Age					
	65+	55–64	45–54	35–44	25–34	18–24
Less than 50,000	46	41	38	23	23	28
50,000 to 199,999	39	38	28	18	13	9
200,000 to 999,999	24	23	32	8	6	5
More than 1 million	29	13	21	5	2	0

Sources: See table 1-2. Those without an opinion are excluded.

Indeed, Lehmann has shown that it is not only current place of residence that correlates with political attitudes, but also the place where a person was born and grew up. As table 1-4 shows, those who were born in the countryside and migrated to the city as adults retained many of the attitudes they had acquired in their village. The younger the age at which they migrated to the city, the more urban their attitudes were as adults. The question used in table 1-4 is merely illustrative: "What do you think about the transition to a market economy in Russia?" The same phenomenon was found in attitudes toward the different parties and in voting behavior. The reader who looks at the total number of respondents in each category will note that more than one-third of the urban population older than age 26 was born in the countryside.

The Psychology of the City and Countryside

One now takes for granted that the larger cities, especially the larger northern cities, have supported radical transformation, while the countryside, especially the rural south, has been a "red belt." Yet one should never forget that this pattern directly contradicted most Western theories advanced during the Brezhnev period about the locus of support and opposition to reform. However the argument was expressed, many argued that those in a privileged position in the old system would be very reluctant to support a radical economic reform that threatened the old institutions or that exposed workers to sharp price increases and unemployment. This implied that the large cities should have been conservative.

Thus when American conservatives talked about the power of the *nomenklatura*, the bureaucrats, or the military-industrial complex, they were talking about the largest cities that were the major defense industry centers and that contained

Table 1-4. Attitudes toward Transition to a Market Economy, by Origin of Respondent, 1993[a]

Percent unless otherwise specified

Origin	Rapid transition	Gradual transition	Against transition	Number of cases
Born rural, living rural[b]	13	56	32	5,886
Migrant, age 23–26[c]	11	56	34	486
Migrant, age 19–22[c]	15	59	27	1,011
Migrant, age 15–18[c]	15	62	23	2,185
Migrant, age 7–14[c]	17	60	23	991
Migrant, age 1–6[c]	17	63	20	730
Born urban, living urban[d]	20	64	16	1,368
Born urban, living urban[e]	22	65	14	1,940
Born urban, living urban[f]	25	64	11	6,337

Sources: See table 1-2.

a. Respondents age 26 or older from the 1993 sample of thirty-four Russian oblasts.

b. Born in a rural place or settlement, currently living in a city of 10,000 or less.

c. Born in a rural place or settlement and migrated to a city at some subsequent point.

d. Born in a small city of up to 50,000 inhabitants, currently living in a city of 50,000 or more.

e. Born in a city of 50,000 to 200,000 inhabitants, currently living in a city of 50,000 or more.

f. Born in a city of more than 200,000 inhabitants, currently living in a city of 50,000 or more.

the largest bureaucratic structures.[11] Others talked about a social contract between regime and workers in which the regime guaranteed workers security and a basically egalitarian society and in return received acquiescence to authoritarian rule.[12] First of all, the scholars had in mind the workers in the major plants of heavy industry and the defense industry.

In general, anyone familiar with life in the Soviet Union knew that quality of life was intimately linked with the size of the city. The larger the city, the better the living conditions. In contrast to the situation in the United States, the Soviet provincial elite—political, economic, and intellectual—was all concentrated in the regional capitals.[13] This concentration ensured that the large centers received the lion's share of resources. Life in small towns and villages in the provinces often seemed a throwback to decades ago.

For all these reasons, if privilege were the crucial factor, those living in large cities should have been disproportionately conservative. Those living in small towns and the countryside should have advocated radical change because they were especially disadvantaged. They should have had a special interest in the kind of economic reform that in its first stages had benefited peasants and rural towns in China.

These generalizations seemed particularly appropriate for the specific type of market reform based on free trade that was to be introduced by Yegor Gaidar. When a country's industry is not competitive, the urban elite and workers usually are strong proponents of a protectionist foreign economic policy. Democracy intensifies rather than removes this political pressure during the early and middle stages of industrialization. This has been shown in the populism and import substitution of Latin American democracy before 1980, the autarkic pressures of democratic India, and the high tariff policy of the U.S. Republican party that won fourteen of eighteen presidential elections from 1860 through 1928.[14] As shown in the United States from 1865 to 1915, Russia from 1890 to 1950, and the Pacific Rim countries after World War II, protectionism at this stage is compatible with high rates of economic growth that continue for decades.

By the same token, rural areas that are competitive in the world market are the natural proponents of free trade because of their interest in lowering the prices of manufactured goods and increasing the amount of money in the hands of foreigners who buy agricultural products.[15] The one region in the United States that consistently favored free trade and voted for the free-trade Democratic party before the 1940s was the South, which depended heavily in those years on the export of cotton and tobacco and had little industry.

This regional and branch pattern was also observed during the great industrialization drive in Russia from 1880 to 1915. The industrializing northern regions supported the protectionism that was part of Count Witte's industrial development program, while the rural south favored free trade. In the crucial days of the 1917 revolution the industrial workers of the northern cities and the peasants working the noncompetitive northern lands supported the Bolsheviks, who rejected the capitalist world economy and market. The peasants of the fertile southern lands voted against the Bolsheviks.[16]

Yet the types of areas that had supported the Communists most fervently in 1917 provided the strongest opposition to them in the late 1980s and early 1990s. Clearly other factors were politically more decisive than basic economic interests, let alone short-range considerations of maintenance of current advantage. These factors were of a psychological or cultural character. If we may be excused for using language that is no longer fashionable, those who lived in the larger cities, especially those born there, turned out to have attitudes that were more modern than the attitudes of those in the countryside and smaller towns.[17] Today it would be more fashionable to call these attitudes the social capital required for maintaining effective democracy.[18] But the factors involved in social capital would look familiar to an older generation using older language.

In other countries, too, people in large cities tend to have a more modern outlook, but the huge difference between the quality of life in Russia's largest cities and its smaller ones gave the talented, the ambitious, and the risk-takers particularly strong incentives to make their way to a large city. In addition, a system of registration (*propiski*) was established to restrict immigration into the largest cities. This system did not prevent the growth of the large cities, but it limited the migrants to those who were most determined and resourceful. Thus instead of big cities becoming dumping grounds for those who could not cope with market forces in the countryside, the farms and smaller cities became resting places for those who did not have the drive and the intelligence to leave.

The inhabitants of the large cities, especially those who were at least second generation urban dwellers, were more tolerant of diversity in views, more willing to take risks, more interested in opportunity than in security. Indeed, they considered the orientation toward security and egalitarianism in communism as primarily benefiting the least efficient and the least adventuresome. They believed they would benefit far more from the market and would be able to tolerate the insecurity it would bring.

This was, of course, particularly true of the young. Children of workers around the world have wanted upward mobility, and Soviet sociological surveys throughout the Brezhnev period showed that parents strongly wanted a college education for their children—a goal that the children, of course, shared. For the young the overstaffing of "the productive sectors" and the starving of the service sector meant a reduction in their opportunities for social mobility.

The inhabitants of the large cities were also culturally different from those in the villages and small towns. The Soviet population had reached levels of education associated with democratization around the world, but those in the large cities were the best educated both formally and informally. Those with whom Westerners had contact in Moscow and St. Petersburg were Western in their views, hungry for more exposure to Western travel and culture. Although Westerners knew few workers in the capital, we saw them wearing blue jeans and listening to rock music on portable radios and recorders. We had little contact with the provinces, but Moscovites claimed the provincials were very provincial. It turned out that this difference was crucial in the politics of the late 1980s and the early 1990s.[19]

The Fatal Flaw in Russian Reform

Boris Yeltsin understood the psychology of the urban dweller in large cities such as Sverdlovsk where he had been party first secretary for a decade. He understood their desire for freedom and opportunity and their tolerance for pain during the transition. Yeltsin had a brilliant political strategy to gain power and maintain it in the short run. Gaidar's deindustrialization strategy produced a 50 percent drop in production, but unemployment was limited by retaining most people in their jobs even if the factory was not producing at full capacity. The groups that bore the brunt of the economic decline—the older and middle-aged, women, and inhabitants of the small towns and countryside—were not those that would go into the streets in protest. Yeltsin's own base of support in the larger cities would be protected. Every effort would be made to split the opposition and to try to demonize the strongest element within it.

If the ideology of the Yeltsin revolution was to be believed, the strategy had every hope of succeeding in the long run as well as the short run. This ideology posited that "reform"—the word "revolution" was never used—was a seamless and unqualified process entailing a pure market and pure democracy. Despite the gradualism that normally is the essence of reform, the introduction of market forces and democracy in Russia had to take place immediately. The old institutions were to be destroyed completely, for otherwise the state (the bureaucrats) would throttle change.[20] A chasm cannot be jumped in two leaps, it was often said, as if the market and democratic institutions existed precreated on the opposite side if only the leap reached them. Both at the time and in retrospect, Russian intellectuals (and Westerners too) spoke of a "500-day plan" that could have achieved full marketization in such a period if only Gorbachev had accepted it.[21] Although not acknowledged as such, the basic assumptions of the revolution were far closer to those of the classics of anarchism than of democracy.

In fact, the process of marketization and the development of well-functioning capitalist institutions takes decades and sometimes centuries. Indeed, the savings and loan debacle in the United States in the 1980s and the debate on out-sourcing in the 1990s shows that the process continues in the most advanced economic systems. A market requires long-term agreements about supplies, financing, and delivery and sale of products. It depends on a reliable legal system and protection of contracts and property, on legal constructs such as the modern corporation. The reason democracies need to worry about overregulation is that the creation of institutions and the establishment of regulation were the first prerequisites of creating a market.

Those shaping American policy toward Russia—they were primarily economists—knew there is a strong statistical link between *democracy*, market economies, and peace, but forgot there is a negative correlation between *democratization*, market economies, and peace.[22] They remembered that the introduction of universal suffrage in Western Europe brought reconciliation of workers with a market economy, but forgot that these workers received the vote not to legitimate the most painful stage of capitalist development, but as an assurance that they would have the power to mitigate that pain through the introduction of social welfare measures. Those associated with international economic institutions knew that newly elected leaders in the third world often have enough legitimacy to introduce painful currency adjustments, but they forgot that this practice requires that the benefits of the pain be plainly visible by the next election.

It is not surprising that neoclassical monetarists do not understand politics or the institutional base of the market. Their work is based on that of economists who worked before the creation of the modern corporation, the modern state, or democratic politics.[23] What is more surprising is that Yeltsin never seems to have understood that the fervor of revolutionary periods passes. Over time, self-interest, and not simply the long-term interest in a brighter future depicted in the new ideology, becomes increasingly important. The consequence of democracy and, indeed, its purpose is to ensure that those who are suffering from a government policy have the opportunity to vote to change it.

Yeltsin seems never to have devoted much thought to the problems of tying mass self-interest to ideology in order to reenforce that ideology. Given the structure of attitudes in Russia at the beginning of the 1990s, he had only to study the history of Russia at the end of nineteenth century and of China in the 1980s. The southern rural areas had a natural interest in economic reform and even free trade: thus it was possible and vital to break the back of the opposition to reform by introducing market pricing for agricultural crops and promoting small-scale private industry in the small towns and cities, as had been done in China. In the short term the higher food prices would have been painful to the urban dwellers, but the strength of their commitment to reform would have carried the regime through the transition period. If the urban workers were promised high tariffs and state sponsorship of investment (not just subsidies for those not working) in the transition period, if they had (in American jargon) been promised job creation and not job destruction, they would have seen confirmation for the optimism that their beliefs had engendered and would have continued to support marketization.

Instead, Yeltsin followed the opposite course. No reform was introduced into agriculture, and the state continued to control wholesale trade in food products. It paid the peasants prices well below market levels, and even these payments were often months late. The state then charged them market prices for machinery, fertilizer, and pesticides, but neither collective farms nor private farmers could afford them. Grain production fell by 50 percent, and conditions in the countryside and small towns worsened. No wonder that their suspicion of economic reform deepened.

Yeltsin further alienated agriculture by compensating for low domestic productivity with foreign imports. Cheap food prices would be guaranteed to his urban constituency with free imports of food. Russian agriculture complained bitterly that these imports were driving down prices for domestic products and even argued that the use of foreign credits to import food amounted to a government subsidy of foreign farmers when Russia's own peasants were suffering.

At the same time, Yeltsin did not invest in the creation of jobs in the large cities, let alone the medium-size ones. In 1994 economists spoke of investment being at 20 percent of the level of the 1980s, and even those who claimed that the economic decline was bottoming out in 1995 with a 4 percent decline in GDP noted that investment was down 12 percent from the depressed 1994 levels.[24]

The two surveys analyzed in this book show the predictable results of Yeltsin's mistakes. The 43 percent of the vote received by the Liberal Democrats, the Communists, and the Agrarians in the 1993 election reflects the very pessimistic attitudes about the policy followed before that time, and events between 1993 and 1995 only compounded the suspicion. In December 1993, 11.0 percent of the population approved completely of Yeltsin's activity as president and an additional 24.1 percent approved on the whole. By December 1995 these figures had fallen to 3.0 percent and 12.6 percent. The share supporting rapid economic reform decreased from 13.3 percent to 6.6 percent. When asked whether they thought the West was attempting to weaken Russia with its economic advice, affirmative answers outnumbered the negative by 2 to 1 in 1993 and 3 to 1 in 1995. A vague question about whether "there exist definite forces who are guilty for the misfortunes of our country" elicited an affirmative response of 4.5 to 1 in 1995.

This startling change of attitudes is also reflected in the increase in the number of people who approved of the Communist party. Of those with an opinion, 23.3

percent approved of the Communists in 1993 and 16.1 percent thought of them more positively than negatively. In 1995, these figures had risen to 31.5 percent and 16.9 percent.

Moreover, 53.4 percent either had not heard of Zyuganov's Communist Party of the Russian Federation in 1993 or had no opinion about it. This figure fell to 30.8 percent in 1995. This meant that the increase in the number of people with a positive opinion of the Communists rose far more rapidly than the approval ratings indicated. Among the 3,900 respondents in the 1993 sample, 713 had a positive or more positive than negative opinion of the Communists; this figure rose to 1,280 among the 3,827 respondents in the 1995 sample. Similarly, the percentage increase in the voting turnout between 1993 and 1995 obscured the scale of the Communist gain: the party went from 12 percent of the vote in 1993 to 22 percent in 1995, an increase from 6,666,402 votes to 15,432,963.

The purpose of this book is to explore these changes in attitude in detail and to try to understand their significance for the outcome of the presidential election of June 1996. With 73 percent of the population disapproving of Yeltsin's performance—44 percent completely disapproving—and 12 percent undecided and two-thirds of the population still disapproving of or uncertain about the Communists, the obvious practical question is which of these two feelings is stronger? Have the Communists reached the limit of their support or do they have a real chance to break through to a 50 percent majority in the presidential runoff?

This book is not the place for a detailed evaluation of the policies that led to such profoundly negative opinions about the reforms in Russia or to the catastrophic collapse in the approval ratings of a man who won 89.6 percent of the vote in Moscow in the 1989 election. But it is the place to raise the policy question and to insist that it be addressed very seriously after the election. Gorbachev and Yeltsin were raised within a system without markets and democratic institutions, and they can certainly be excused for not understanding the complex nature of democracy, the relation between democracy and the free market, and the relation between democracy and foreign economic policy. But they were encouraged by the West in all their worst and most naive mistakes.

When three-quarters of the Russian public thinks the West has been trying to weaken Russia with its economic advice and more than 60 percent thinks that "there exist definite forces" (in the minds of many, no doubt, associated with an international banking conspiracy of ancient lore) who are responsible for Russia's misfortunes, it is time for the West to give serious thought to policy. The explanation for the Western economic advice, despite the suspicion of the average Russian, was not a desire to weaken Russia, but ideological blindness among advisers desperately eager for economic reform in Russia to succeed.

But sincerity does not guarantee good results. If war is too important to leave to generals, foreign economic policy is too important to leave to economists without any knowledge of the role of institutions in economic life or the relationship between democratization, marketization, and questions of war and peace. This is an issue to which scholars must give great thought in the coming years.

2

Boris Yeltsin and Economic Reform

The 1995 Duma election marked the seventh time Russian voters went to the polls in as many years, and, one way or another, Boris Yeltsin had been a key figure each time. After being elected the first president of Russia in June 1991, he was instrumental in breaking up the Soviet Union and launching a radical economic reform. Although he was not on the ballot in 1995 and did not associate himself with any political party, the election still was largely a referendum on him and his policies.

Yeltsin and the Congress of People's Deputies

Americans have always seen Russian politics through the eyes of the radical Moscow intellectuals. At any specific time, these intellectuals' interpretation of events has reflected the political needs of those they were supporting. Because their political allegiance has frequently shifted, so too has their interpretation, often to the point of flatly contradicting a previous position. The West has been left with a jumble of inconsistent memories.

Thus, before 1990 Mikhail Gorbachev was the hero of the intellectuals, who described him as a radical economic reformer and portrayed the bureaucrats as conservative opponents of reform (it turns out from memoirs that Gorbachev was sabotaging the serious efforts at economic reform of premier Nikolai Ryzhkov and his team of bureaucrats).[1] In 1990 the intellectuals shifted allegiance to Boris Yeltsin. They said Yeltsin backed radical economic reform and Gorbachev had turned against it. Yet Gorbachev was finally adopting radical reform measures, while Yeltsin was taking a populist position through a reckless expansion of the money supply and a simultaneous denunciation of all price increases.

In 1994 and 1995 Yeltsin turned against the intellectuals, and they began denouncing him as a coarse and authoritarian political ruler. Yet his political style and behavior remained what it had been from 1991 to 1993 when they were hailing him as the embodiment of democracy and condemning the Congress of People's Deputies as an undemocratic tool of the *nomenklatura*. The bureaucrats, the intellectuals said, had taken control of privatization ("*nomenklatura* privatization" was the term used) but still opposed economic reform and wanted to return to the old system. This suggested either that the bureaucrats were remarkably selfless or that something was seriously wrong with the analysis.

If one is to understand Russian politics during the past few years, one must try to cut through the mythology. The Soviet managerial class was not privileged under socialism but very underprivileged by Western standards, and it has benefited enormously from economic reform. Not surprisingly, Soviet managers remain strong supporters of reform, although, of course, like Western businessmen and managers, they see nothing inconsistent between capitalism as a system and concrete tariffs and subsidies that benefit them personally. As table 2-1 shows, they were the group that was most supportive of the privatization of large enterprises in 1993, other than private businessmen, and this remained true in our 1995 survey.

Boris Yeltsin has been difficult to understand not simply because his supporters deliberately misrepresented him from 1990 to 1994, but because he has a very unusual combination of political characteristics. He has always seen politics not as a coalitional process aimed at achieving policy goals but as a zero-sum game of personal struggle for power. And he has been utterly single-minded in his drive for power. Sensing he could take over Gorbachev's position by abolishing his country and that neither Gorbachev nor the military would effectively resist, he pushed ahead without hesitation, even though he probably would have lost his life if he had misjudged either one. He was willing to make any promise and conclude any deal and then within days or weeks openly violate it without apology. He found it extremely difficult to cooperate with anyone as an equal. In these senses he has been authoritarian in dominating the political process.

Yet, despite his political ruthlessness, Yeltsin has treated politics as a game. His memoirs attest to his love of volleyball and tennis, but they say little about policy preferences. This reflects his approach to politics. In a game one does not kill or imprison opponents, and Yeltsin has never used repression against political foes, let alone the entire population. He even acquiesced in the release

Table 2-1. Attitude toward Privatization of Large Enterprises, by Occupation, 1993, 1995

Percent

Occupation	1993			1995		
	Favor	Oppose	Don't know	Favor	Oppose	Don't know
Private business	57	23	19	48	30	22
Upper manager	53	34	12	43	56	1
Middle manager	41	44	13	26	58	16
Professional	45	36	18	24	51	25
White collar	43	33	23	21	55	24
Worker	41	35	24	19	54	27
Peasant	23	48	28	14	50	34
Sample	41	36	22	22	52	25

Sources: See table 1-2.

of those who attempted coups against him—including Vice President Aleksandr Rutskoi who called on demonstrators to seize the television station in Moscow and thereby provoked an armed conflict that resulted in hundreds of deaths. In these ways Yeltsin has been nonauthoritarian. Indeed, he deserves severe criticism for the opposite behavior, for not setting up a strong administrative and legal system that functions effectively.

These contradictory features of Yeltsin's political personality were crucial in the conflict between him and the Russian Congress of People's Deputies. Although Yeltsin was later to denounce the Congress as undemocratic and dominated by the Communist *nomenklatura*, the 1990 election for the legislature represented a major advance over the 1989 elections for the USSR legislature and were free.[2] Some 40 percent of the deputies supported rapid and even radical reform, 35 to 40 percent were conservative, and 20 to 25 percent were centrist. The reform and conservative camps themselves were each divided into hardliners and moderates.

As a result, Yeltsin was able to win on a number of key issues in the Russian Congress in 1990 and 1991. The first Congress elected him to the most important post in the republic—chairman of the Supreme Soviet, the legislative body that met between congressional sessions—and it passed a Declaration of Sovereignty that proclaimed Russian laws superseded USSR laws. In May 1991 it agreed by a two-thirds majority to create the post of Russian president, knowing that Yeltsin was certain to be elected (he was elected in June).

When Yeltsin and the Russian Congress were elected, almost everyone expected that the Soviet Union would continue to exist in some form. In March 1991 more than 70 percent of Russian voters agreed in a referendum that the Union of Soviet Socialist Republics should become a reformed federation, and many, if not most, of the negative votes were cast because of the implication of the name that socialism was being approved. When the presidency was created, the Yeltsin forces agreed to reverse their position on the supremacy of USSR laws over Russian laws. Yeltsin himself supported the preservation of the union, albeit a modified one, during his campaign for president.

Partly for this reason, Russia had a very unnatural political structure when it became independent. The hurried introduction of a presidency in Russia in May 1991 had created an uneasy relationship between the Congress and president. As in the French system, the premier was subordinate both to the president and Congress, but unlike the French (or American) system, the Congress did not have the right to confirm individual cabinet officers. Little attention was paid to details because it was assumed that a central government in some form would restrain Yeltsin's power.

When the August 1991 coup d'etat failed and the USSR government began to disintegrate, the Russian Congress decided to grant Yeltsin emergency powers for a year. He was permitted to appoint regional governors so he could replace those leaders who had supported the coup. He was also allowed to issue decrees on economic reform in his own name. Again, because the law could be repealed in a year, contentious issues were solved by unwritten gentlemen's agreements, which Yeltsin later often failed to observe.

Once Russia became independent, everyone agreed that the new country needed a new constitution and new elections to give its officials legitimacy. The Congress, however, wanted a constitution that delineated presidential powers similar to those in the old constitution or perhaps with an even stronger system of checks and balances. Yeltsin naturally wanted the new constitution to incorporate the emergency powers he was already exercising. The existing constitution gave the Congress the exclusive right to amend the constitution, and the Congress wanted to use this procedure to introduce a new constitution either all at once or in parts. Yeltsin wanted a constitutional convention in which he selected the delegates.

The opposing interests of Yeltsin and the Congress made conflict inevitable, but Yeltsin's style of leadership intensified it. He had treated Gorbachev with ill-disguised contempt, and now he did the same with the leaders of the Congress, most of whom had been mere college professors in early 1990. Yeltsin delighted in acting in a way that not only aggrandized power to himself but publicly dramatized what he was doing.

While the Congress could not confirm cabinet officers, it retained the right to confirm the premier. However, Yeltsin circumvented this right in November 1991 by naming himself premier and making the real occupant of this post, Gennady Burbulis, first deputy premier, a post not subject to Congress's confirmation. In his memoirs he confirmed what was obvious at the time, that he had done so to deprive the Congress of its constitutional right to vote on Burbulis.[3] When Yeltsin stepped aside as premier in April 1992 and removed Burbulis as first deputy premier, he again avoided the confirmation process by naming Yegor Gaidar acting premier.

Yeltsin also pursued an economic policy that, whether inherently desirable or not, was certain to exacerbate relations with any elected legislature. After attacking Gorbachev for introducing price increases, he himself introduced a policy that produced more than 2,000 percent inflation in the first year alone. In November 1991 he had predicted that production would increase once more in the fall of 1992, but it fell 19 percent during the year and showed no sign of stabilizing. Finally, as shall be seen, he put a large portion of government expenditures off budget and thereby deprived the Congress of any meaningful power over the budget.

The deputies criticized Yeltsin's policies and blamed his government (although seldom Yeltsin personally) for the unpredicted painful consequences. Indeed, because Yeltsin and the Congress agreed that a new constitution (and therefore elections) was needed quickly, the deputies had little choice but to dissociate themselves from the unpopular reform being followed. Yeltsin was strongly tempted to use the Congress as the scapegoat for Russia's problems. As economic conditions worsened, the criticism both of and by the Congress intensified and became increasingly emotional.

The Gaidar Economic Strategy

Compared with other countries, the Soviet Union had far too many people employed in industry and far too few in the service sector for its stage of economic development.[4] Observers agreed that structural change—deindustrialization—was a crucial element of reform. The Chinese had allowed the private service sector to grow up around the state sector and gradually draw off state workers by offering higher wages. Mancur Olson had argued in *The Rise and*

Decline of Nations that the revolutionary destruction of old institutions and the creation of new ones on the rubble was far more effective than an attempt to reform old ones.[5] This argument was influential both with the economists in international institutions in Washington and with important figures in the Gaidar entourage. Gaidar had cited Olson extensively in his doctoral dissertation.

Proponents of shock therapy saw sudden deindustrialization as far more effective and less painful than gradual reform. Immediate release of controls on prices and the destruction of the Soviet Union and its institutions were defended as the best way to clear the way for new institutions. Inefficient plants would be forced to close, and managers in other plants would be compelled to lay off unneeded workers. The unemployed would be forced to move into the under-staffed service sector simply to survive. Market prices would ensure that everyone would be responding to the correct economic signals about their behavior in the new situation. Policy was based on a deep faith in monetarist theory. It was thought that if the money supply were brought under control, this alone would limit price increases to a few hundred percent.

This is not the place for a critique of the ideology underlying the Gaidar economic reform, but it had two obvious political problems. First, fifty years of centrally dictated economic policy had resulted in too many of the most talented and ambitious people in Soviet society becoming workers, engineers, and managers in industry, especially in heavy industry and the defense industry. These were, of course, the very people the radical marketizers would want forced into the new private sector. Politically this meant that in the short and medium term most of the talented and ambitious were employed in sectors slated for immediate destruction by the new regime. The armed forces that would be required to suppress unrest could not themselves have wanted the destruction of the defense industry that was producing unrest. These two facts, taken together, created an obvious political problem.

Second, the non-Russian republics all depended on Russia for petroleum, natural gas, and other raw materials. If these products were suddenly priced at world market levels, these republics would not be able to afford them and their economies would collapse. Twenty-five million Russians lived in the non-Rus-sian republics, the great majority in cities, and were employed in industry. The sudden collapse of industry would provoke either revolt or massive migration, and both would create irresistible political pressure in Russia for action.

The Yeltsin regime adopted a creative solution to this problem.[6] In 1990 and 1991 under Gorbachev, the Soviet industrial ministries were being transformed into so-called private holding companies, firms, corporations, and the like. An industrial bank was created for each ministry and made responsible for handling the banking activities for it and its enterprises, including the provision of loans. Clearly a transition to market-driven activity was being envisaged in which government investment would be directed to quasi-governmental holding companies through quasi-governmental banks. In time both would become increasingly independent of government.

These institutions were retained by the Yeltsin government and were directly supervised by the Ministry of Industry and the Ministry of Finance. The holding companies and corporations served as "wholesale trading agencies" that provided their enterprises, many of them in the non-Russian republics, with supplies. The industrial banks provided the enterprises with loans to finance their operations.

Yeltsin supporters and their spokesmen in America blamed the money creation and the inflation associated with it on the State Bank, which was subordinated to the Congress, and on loans among the enterprises. This was a gross misrepresentation of the facts. "Interenterprise loans" (nonpayment of bills) might explain how enterprises were obtaining supplies, but it could not explain where they were acquiring the hard cash to pay workers and taxes. These were being financed by "loans" from the industrial banks, and these "loans" reflected decisions by the executive. The State Bank created the money needed to finance the payment of wages and taxes, but it was required to do so. The chairman of the State Bank, Viktor Gerashchenko, was retained not only after the dissolution of the Congress, but even after the State Bank was officially subordinated to the executive following promulgation of the new constitution. He was personally close to Premier Chernomydin and had the highest reputation in the West in 1990.[7]

The Gaidar government was actually following a fairly sophisticated policy. There was no unemployment insurance system, and the retention of workers by the enterprises was the only effective way to provide a social safety net, all the more so because the enterprises always provided many social services to their workers. In sectors in which the regime was trying to cut back on production (the defense industry, for example), wages were set at low levels to try to force workers to seek employment in the private sector or the service industries. If the economy turned around in a year or two as expected, the combination of a cushion for unemployment and an incentive to move into the service sector was reasonable.

The policy was, however, implemented in a very dishonest manner. The government should have appropriated money for the subsidies, no doubt with a

Keynesian explanation about the need for deficits to maintain purchasing power during depressions. By relying on "interenterprise loans" (a large portion of them from the state-owned oil and gas companies) and unacknowledged industrial bank "loans," the government put the deficits off-budget. Even more astonishing, local government was being financed largely by a tax on the profits of socialist enterprises. The enterprises were cutting production sharply and retaining their labor force, but were making enough profits to keep local government budgets balanced as they soared with inflation.

In February 1993 the head of the Central Bank, Viktor Gerashchenko, spoke frankly to leaders of the local soviets about the planned budget deficit of 3.5 trillion rubles and the "hidden part" of the budget of 6 trillion rubles to be financed by credit. "The reason for this dual bookkeeping," he said, "is the dependence of the Russians on the international financial institutions who make a budgetary deficit not larger than 5 percent of gross national product a condition for western help."[8] When the history of the period is written, it will be interesting to learn whether the international economic community was as completely naive as it seemed or whether it was insisting on fraudulent figures for its own purposes.

In any case the result was lethal for the smooth development of democracy in Russia. Because the off-budget expenditures were the crucial marginal ones and the Congress had little effect on them, it essentially lost its power over the budget. The international agencies may not have understood the political implications of off-budget financing, but the Yeltsin government surely did. This situation was the major cause of the Congress's bitterness toward the government, especially since it was being blamed for fueling inflation.

In addition, despite the talk about market-set prices and a money-supply explanation for inflation, the quasi-governmental corporations, holding companies, and banks had fairly firm control of prices. A major reason for rapid inflation, as local officials in the city of Yaroslavl explained, was the need to keep prices rising so that the enterprises would have the "profits" needed to pay their taxes.

A broader political strategy was also involved. The large cities were the center of Yeltsin's support, while the villages and small towns were the strongest supporters of the opposition. The cities were centers of defense industry production, and they would have suffered most from Gaidar's deindustrialization program had it not been for the decision to limit unemployment, continue paying nonproducers, and provide foreign consumer goods for them. The regime was determined not to destroy its base of political support.

But if production is down sharply, the major industrial centers are being subsidized, and a class of new Russian rich is being formed, something or someone has to suffer. In the first two years, consumption was protected to a considerable extent by a reduction in investment and defense expenditures, as well as by loans from the West to purchase consumer goods for the major cities. When the income figures in the 1993 survey are examined, many groups in society seemed to be treated equitably. Employment rates and income seemed fairly constant in cities larger than 25,000 people and, at least among men, in all age groups younger than age 50 (see tables 3-4 and 3-5).

But several groups clearly bore the brunt of economic reform. First, in October 1993 working women were earning 59,700 rubles a month in their basic job compared with 89,300 rubles a month for working men.[9] Second, men 50 years of age and older earned 72,000 rubles in their basic job, while those younger than 50 earned 93,200 rubles. Data were not collected on pensions, but by all evidence retirees were doing very poorly. Third, those in agriculture and small towns earned much less than others. Working men living in towns and villages of less than 25,000 persons earned 60,200 rubles a month compared with 106,600 rubles for those living in larger towns and in cities.

Clearly the decision being made was that women, people older than 50, and those working in agriculture and living in small towns were not politically dangerous. In the short run the calculation was correct: revolutions are not made by women, the middle-aged, or citizens of small towns. However, these groups do vote. Women living with husbands or sons could rely on their salaries; there was no gender gap in their voting behavior that reflected the salary differentials. However, people older than 50 and those living in smaller towns did not have this protection, and they voted heavily for the Communists and the Liberal Democrats of Vladimir Zhirinovsky in the 1993 election. Those living in towns and cities with less than 100,000 people included more than half the population in Russia. If policy toward them did not improve, their unhappiness was certain to increase.

Toward Confrontation

Yeltsin and Gaidar were far too optimistic in their early predictions about inflation and the timing of an upturn in production. By April 1992 the moderates in the Congress had joined with the conservatives in calling for policy change. Yeltsin made some concessions, but when he appointed Gaidar acting premier in June, he indicated that the basic policy was not going to be changed. The legislative leaders did not seriously object. Yeltsin's emergency powers were to expire at the end of the year, he and Gaidar had promised improvement by then, and the Congress would be able to vote on Gaidar and on Yeltsin's emergency powers at that time. They were content to wait.

Boris Yeltsin also seemed to have every reason to change course at the end of 1992. To a large extent the inflation and fall in production in 1992 were the inevitable consequence of the destruction of the USSR government. There were no effective institutions to conduct a subtle policy of regulation even if such a policy were desired. Many of the key members of the Gaidar government were economists in their thirties and early forties without administrative experience—"little boys in pink trousers, red shirts, and yellow shoes," Vice President Aleksandr Rutskoi called them derisively.[10] Their assumption that experienced civil servants were conservative bureaucrats led to a strong disinclination to use them. This made the situation even more ungovernable than was inherently necessary.

But if Yeltsin's support of Gaidar was an inevitable result of breaking up the Soviet Union and replacing Gorbachev, a new administrative structure had been built by the end of 1992. The early promises of the radicals had been shown to be overly optimistic. Yeltsin's obvious political strategy was to use Gaidar as a scapegoat and agree with the Congress on a premier who would move towards a state-directed industrial policy and something more like the Chinese model of economic reform.

The Congress was even ready to vote for Gaidar if he would change his policy, and the early negotiations between Gaidar and the moderates seemed promising. The Congress voted against Gaidar's nomination by a surprisingly close 486 to 467, and the stage seemed set for a compromise in which Gaidar would appoint a number of ministers acceptable to the moderates and would change his policy. But on December 10 Yeltsin went to the Congress and denounced the legislators in the harshest terms. He called for a referendum in which the people would choose between the president and the Congress.

After a few days of extreme tension in which the military and security forces pledged to support the constitution, Yeltsin and the legislators reached a compromise. Viktor Chernomyrdin, the last Soviet minister of the gas industry under Gorbachev, was appointed premier and confirmed. The Congress renewed Yeltsin's emergency powers and agreed to a vague referendum on the constitution. Yeltsin agreed that appointments of "power ministers"—defense, foreign affairs, state security, and internal affairs—would be subject to legislative confirmation.

Chernomyrdin pledged to emphasize the restoration of industrial production, and he issued a decree freezing a number of prices. The moderates understood they had a pledge that he would appoint moderate ministers in the coming months. But nothing changed. The important deputy premiers on economic reform were retained, and the new deputy premier for finances and economics—the de facto replacement for Gaidar—was Boris Fedorov, Russia's representative to the World Bank and an economist more radical than Gaidar.

Fedorov's first act was to announce that Chernomyrdin's decree on price controls did not represent government policy. In fact, it was annulled. The fiscal policy of the Chernomyrdin government became tighter than Gaidar's, and production fell sharply in the first six months of 1993. Moreover, Chernomyrdin was more selective in his subsidies, placing real pressure on plants not thought to have a future to reduce their labor forces sharply.

As president, Yeltsin had the power to appoint cabinet officers; at the time the press reported that Chernomyrdin was powerless and was being overruled. In retrospect, it seems more important that he came from the oil and gas industries that benefited from shock therapy. When a decision was made to privatize them, he became an enthusiastic supporter of the strategy. It was widely assumed that privatization of the gas industry made him one of the most wealthy men in Russia.

The likely explanation for Yeltsin's choice is psychological: for whatever reason, he had decided that the issue was a contest of will and power between the Congress and himself rather than between the Congress and the radicals in his government.

The Congress was, of course, thoroughly frustrated. It thought it had won a moderation of economic policy, but instead policy became more radical. At its next session, in March 1993, it annulled the decision to give Yeltsin emergency powers by a 623 to 382 vote, with the moderates joining the conservatives to annul. Yeltsin responded by imposing "temporary" presidential rule. The Congress made an effort to impeach him, but the 617 to 269 vote showed that Yeltsin's opponents were more than 70 votes short of the number needed for such drastic action against the president.[11]

In the deadlock another compromise was tried. The Congress agreed to a four-question referendum that gave Yeltsin much of what he wanted. The population was asked whether it trusted the president and whether it wanted elections for the Congress and president to be held before they were scheduled. The congressional leaders had been taunting Yeltsin, challenging him to put his economic and social policy to a vote. He agreed. The leaders hoped that the people would express their trust in the president, thereby assuaging his insecurity, but would reject his economic policy and give him a face-saving reason to change it. The legislators also wanted new elections of the legislature and the president, confident that Yeltsin would be reelected, that the balance of forces in the legislature would remain much the same, and that a premier acceptable to the Congress would be appointed.

The leaders of the Congress badly miscalculated. As expected, 58.7 percent of those voting in the referendum expressed trust in the president. With both the pro-Congress and pro-presidential forces calling for new congressional elections, they were supported by 67.2 percent of the voters, but with the two forces split on the presidential election, only officially 49.4 percent of the population voted for presidential elections, although 34,017,310 people favored new presidential elections and only 32,418,972 were opposed.[12] But to the shock of the Congress, 53.1 percent voted in favor of Yeltsin's social and economic policy. The votes in the referendum were nonbinding, but they had a major psychological impact on the opposition.

Yeltsin now acted decisively. In May, he called for a constitutional convention to be held in June, with delegates to be selected in a way his supporters could control. The convention included more than 1,000 participants, but the real drafting was done by a small inner circle working behind closed doors. The constitution that emerged featured a dominant president. In September, Yeltsin dissolved the Congress and set new legislative elections and a referendum on the new constitution for December.

According to the existing constitution, any branch of government that dissolved another automatically removed itself from power. Yeltsin therefore officially forfeited his presidency by his action, and Vice President Rutskoi automatically became president. Rutskoi proclaimed himself president and was supported by the Congress. For fourteen days, Russia had two presidents, one who more or less controlled the country and the other who controlled the parliament building, the White House.

Once again, the military remained neutral, and after ten days, it appeared that a compromise might be reached on simultaneous presidential and legislative elections. But on October 4 several thousand demonstrators under reactionary leadership broke through poorly defended police barricades, occupied the parliament building, and seized the mayor's office next door to it. Rutskoi called on the demonstrators to seize the television station and, in a bloody battle, they almost succeeded. It was this action that led to the shelling of the parliament that was seen around the world on television. Again, the military refused to become involved. Even Alfa, the elite division of the security forces, would not storm the parliament building. But Yeltsin persuaded its commander to try to bluff its occupiers by marching in front of it. Only when a sniper killed an Alfa soldier did Alfa become angry enough to attack the building.

It was a remarkable series of events: the fate of one of the world's two superpowers turned on the actions of a few thousand demonstrators, incompetent police crowd control, and a single division of the country's armed forces that itself was not under effective central control.

3

The 1993 Election and Its Aftermath

The showdown between Yeltsin and the Congress in the fall of 1993 left Russian politics in a shambles. A referendum for a new constitution was scheduled for December 12, but so too were the elections for the new legislature. Deputies therefore had to be elected to a legislature that had not been created, and because no legislature existed, no election law could be passed. Yeltsin introduced new electoral rules by decree, and the nonexistent legislative institutions for which candidates were nominated were those proposed in the new constitution on the referendum ballot.

The 1993 elections were held in great haste. Yeltsin dissolved the old parliament on September 21. On October 5, after using tanks to blast the Russian White House, he succeeded in arresting parliament's defenders. Parties and blocs had a little more than one month to collect the signatures necessary to be placed on the ballot. The final slate of organizations and candidates contesting the election was determined on November 12. This allowed one month for the actual campaign.

Few parties had a chance to establish their image or message in any meaningful way. Even at the end of the campaign, 44 percent of respondents in our 1993 survey stated that they had not seen any election posters the previous seven days, and 44 percent said they had seen only a few. Twenty-seven percent denied that they had heard anything about the Communist Party of the the Russian Federation, and 22 percent of those who had heard of it said they could not evaluate it.[1] It seemed ludicrous for Russians to say they had not heard of the Communist party, but, in fact, there were five Communist parties, and many people had little conception of which one was Zyuganov's.

The Duma that emerged from the 1993 election contained 179 deputies in conservative parties and factions, 103 in centrist ones, 100 in radical ones, and 57 in rapid reform ones. The Duma thus had a political balance similar to the old Congress, although with a slight increase in the relative weight of the conservative deputies. A leader of the old Communists of Russia faction in the Congress, Ivan Rybkin, was elected chairman of the Duma.

Most moderate and conservative leaders decided to avoid frontal confrontation with Yeltsin and the Chernomyrdin government. Yeltsin had succeeded in making the Congress of People's Deputies the scapegoat for economic difficulties between 1991 and 1993, and the new legislative leaders were determined to act in a way that made the president and his government completely responsible for the course of events between 1993 and 1995. They bet that the population would be deeply unhappy by the results of policy, and in this they bet correctly.

The 1993 Election

The new legislature was a National Assembly with two independent houses: a Duma of 450 deputies to represent the population and a Federation Council of 178 deputies to represent the country's 89 regions. Half the Duma deputies were chosen in a party list election and distributed by proportional representation, and half were elected in districts with more or less equal numbers of electors.[2] Duma was the name of the weak legislature established by Tsar Nicholas II after the Revolution of 1905, and no doubt the use of the word in 1993 was meant to recall the earlier institution. Indeed, the Duma that convened in January 1994 was even labeled "the Fifth Duma," a phrase that stressed the continuities with the prerevolutionary institutions.

According to the new constitution, the deputies to the Federation Council were to be "selected," and it was expected that the executive and legislature in each of the 89 regions would each select one deputy. In fact, the deputies were expected to be the governor and the chairman of the regional legislative body, and the council was expected to meet only periodically. But because Yeltsin had dissolved many of the regional legislatures, few chairmen would exist in December 1993, so it was necessary to elect the Federation Council deputies by popular vote.[3]

The use of a variant of the German electoral law for selecting Duma deputies served two interests: the party list system that was elected by proportional representation guaranteed seats for Moscow politicians associated with the major parties, while the individual districts would ensure regional representation. The academics drafting the law also understood that the logic of the system led toward the formation of the kind of party system dominated by two parties that was found in Germany, and they hoped this would occur in Russia as well. Obviously, proportional representation requires the creation of parties, but seats would be awarded only to parties that received 5 percent or more of the vote. District elections to the old Congress of People's Deputies had featured a runoff if no candidate received a majority in the first round, but now the candidate with a plurality in the first round was declared the victor. Both the 5 percent minimum requirement and the plurality rule in the districts, it was hoped, would create powerful incentives for parties to coalesce before the election.[4]

The suddenness of the election, however, and the haste with which it was conducted left little time for planning or coalescence. It was even unclear which parties would be allowed to run. Although the Constitutional Court had overturned Yeltsin's 1991 ban on the Communist party, the Communists and their allies had supported the Congress in the September 1993 showdown with Yeltsin. Initially Zyuganov's Communists were banned along with more hardline groups, but a presidential decree of October 18 allowed them to participate. Some of the more hard-line groups remained barred.

Although allowed on the ballot, the Communist party had little money for its campaign. Its national headquarters were housed in a very small free office, located in a building with space set aside for social organizations. Virtually all its campaign material was typed on a conventional typewriter and copied rather than printed. The party relied extensively on 3" × 5" slips of paper that supporters distributed on strategic corners. Posters were almost nonexistent, and the party had little access to television. Its main newspaper, *Pravda,* was shut down in the aftermath of Yeltsin's confrontation with parliament and was allowed to publish only after November 2. The paper appeared for just two weeks before it ceased publication, this time for lack of funds. It did not reappear until December 10, two days before the election.

Our survey at the time of the 1993 election showed that Russian public opinion was reasonably centrist in its preference for a policy of gradual economic reform and a tolerant confederation of the republics of the former Soviet Union. But credible leaders did not have time to form centrist parties, let alone coalesce into large, broad parties that could function as governing coalitions after the election. Ruslan Khasbulatov and Aleksandr Rutskoi were the only charismatic leaders of the centrist and mildly nationalist forces, but they were in jail and were not permitted to participate in the election.[5]

Thirteen parties were successful in obtaining enough valid signatures to be registered. But most centrist parties were unknown to voters, and only Women of Russia and the Democratic Party of Russia were able to break the 5 percent threshold. Women of Russia did surprisingly well with 8.1 percent of the total vote and 15 percent of women's votes, but it received little support from men.[6] The Agrarian party, which was the party of the peasants, allied itself closely with the Communists. It further confused its image by putting top governmental officials at the head of its ticket, thereby seeming to assume responsibility for the agricultural policy it was condemning.

A number of "reform" political parties were formed. The most important was Russia's Choice, headed by first deputy premier Yegor Gaidar. It was frankly described as "the government party," and the top of its list was filled with government ministers. Various satellite opposition parties were also formed. One was a complete misrepresentation—the Russian Party of Unity and Accord (PRES), which claimed to be pro-regions and moderate. It was led by Sergei Shakhrai, Yeltsin's legal adviser and the strongest centralizer in his entourage, and Aleksandr Shokhin, the radical deputy premier who was Gaidar's closest associate in economic reform. Gregory Yavlinsky established an anti-Gaidar party (Yabloko) that basically favored radical economic reform but was antagonistic to Gaidar as a personal rival. An earlier political generation of reformers, including the mayor of St. Petersburg and Gorbachev's chief adviser, Aleksandr Yakovlev, formed the Russian Movement for Democratic Reform.

Leaders of the Congress had miscalculated in early 1993 in assuming the public would vote solidly against Yeltsin's economic and social policies in the April 1993 referendum. The radicals erred just as grievously in assuming the results were an endorsement of shock therapy rather than of Yeltsin's populist measures on the eve of the referendum. Yegor Gaidar sought an unambiguous mandate for his policies. In the two months before the election he increased bread prices, promised drastic new price increases and reductions of subsidies after the election, and even withheld wages to workers and soldiers and payments to peasants for their harvest as a way to reduce the money supply and inflationary pressures.

This was hardly a traditional preelection strategy, but those associated with Gaidar, including his Western advisers, were supremely confident he and his allies would win a majority in the new Duma. Pro-government polling agencies had predicted that he would receive between 25 and 40 percent of the vote. It was assumed that the three satellite parties would each pick up a different segment of the vote and would vote together with Russia's Choice on key issues in the Duma. The abolition of the runoff in single-member districts was expected to lead to a sweep for Gaidar's party if it won its anticipated 25 to 40 percent of the vote. The radicals were so confident of victory that they scheduled a victory celebration on state television, and the broadcast began before the votes were counted. The television program turned out to be even more memorable than expected as cameras focused on the faces of the party-goers as the votes came in.

In fact, Gaidar's party, Russia's Choice, received only 15.5 percent of the party list vote, while the other three radical parties together received only 18.7 percent of the vote. The Russian Movement for Democratic Reform and several other small parties on this part of the spectrum failed to reach the 5 percent minimum. Thus the radicals and rapid reform parties together received only 30 percent of the party list deputies. Deputies of like persuasion won seats in 35 percent of the 225 single-member districts. Centrist parties won 16 percent of the vote and a comparable number of seats in the party list. Candidates that joined centrist parties and factions won 30 percent of the seats in the single-member districts.

The three conservative parties—the Communists, the Agrarians, and the Liberal Democrats of Vladimir Zhirinovsky—won 43 percent of the vote in party elections as a whole. But because no conservative party received less than 5 percent of the vote, the three gained from the redistribution of the votes of small parties on other parts of the spectrum and won 50 percent of the seats selected by party list. They did less well in the single-member districts, however, winning only 30 percent of these seats. The Communists and the Agrarian party together won 19 percent of single-member seats—appropriate for their combined party vote—but the Liberal Democrats won only 2 percent.

Despite his poor showing in the district elections, the surprise beneficiary of the snap election was Vladimir Zhirinovsky and his Liberal Democratic party. As a complete unknown, Zhirinovsky had done unexpectedly well in the 1991 presidential election, receiving 7 percent of the vote. His 1991 campaign had combined extreme nationalism with some bizarre proposals (for example, free beer for everyone), and in 1993 he was the best-financed opposition candidate. In his early career he had held a series of minor jobs usually reserved for KGB agents, and rumors swirled that the KGB or the government or both were providing him with money in order to take votes from the more serious opposition parties—the Communists and the Agrarians.

Whatever Zhirinovsky's source of financing, he and Gaidar dominated television coverage of the campaign. He proved a highly skilled television campaigner, and in an election in which many voters (especially in villages, towns, and small cities) received little information other than from television, he often was perceived as the only way to protest government policy. He received

22.9 percent of the vote, with there being a major shift in the late voting intentions of those without interest in politics but who watched television frequently (table 3-1).

Thus, as a result of the dissolution of the Congress, the successors to the Democratic Russia coalition that had 40 percent of the deputies elected in 1990 fell to 35 percent in 1993. The conservative successors to the Communists of Russia expanded slightly to 40 percent, while the centrists had 25 percent. The overall political balance remained not far from what it had been since 1990.

Yeltsin had always portrayed Russian politics as a conflict between his supporters and the Communists, and his supporters now extended this image in speaking about a Red-Brown (communist- fascist) coalition that had led to a further disappearance of the center in the 1993 election. Pro-Yeltsin analysts exaggerated their point by ignoring the large number of centrist candidates elected in the districts, but by any standards, a 35 percent–25 percent–40 percent division between radical, centrist, and conservative was scarcely a classic bell-shaped curve.

Post-1993 Economic Policy and Its Consequences

The vote for Vladimir Zhirinovsky in the 1993 Duma election, it was correctly said at the time, was largely meant as a protest. The Communists emphasized economic issues and adopted a very hard-line position. They received an appropriate number of votes for the percentage of voters strongly opposed to economic reform. Zhirinovsky's voters, by contrast, were relatively moderate, and most were not voting for fascism, but for the one strong opposition party that favored moderate economic reform.

The purpose of a protest vote is to send a message to political powers. Yet when Yegor Gaidar was removed as deputy premier and Boris Fedorov as minister of finance in early 1994, Premier Viktor Chernomyrdin generally continued the policy they had advocated. Monetary policy continued to be tightened, and the rate of inflation fell from 940 percent in 1993 to 315 percent in 1994 and 131 percent in 1995. The government became more selective in its subsidies, allowing some plants to shut down for a long time. Production fell sharply in the first half of the year, and the decline for all of 1994 was officially put at 12 percent.

Statistics on gross domestic product in Russia are highly controversial. Soviet GDP figures were always difficult to compare with those in the West because of different bases of pricing in centralized and market economic systems.[7] After

Table 3-1. Voting Intention among Frequent Television Watchers, by Level of Interest in Politics, Last Two Weeks of November and First Two Weeks of December, 1993

Percent

	Party intend to vote for		
Level of interest	Liberal Democrats	Communists	Gaidar
No interest, last two weeks of November	13	14	14
No interest, first two weeks of December	23	8	16
High interest, last two weeks of November	13	15	22
High interest, first two weeks of December	17	13	21

Sources: See table 1-2.

1991 Russia partly changed the basis of pricing and experienced extraordinary rates of inflation and artificial exchange rates, all of which increased the problems of measuring gross domestic product. Data on activity in the private sector are highly unreliable, and the State Statistical Agency estimates value through "expert evaluation." The government has little incentive to underestimate, but domestic and foreign supporters of government policy claim, although without citing evidence, that it does so. The claim seems unlikely. When a decrease of production is acknowledged, it is sometimes said to be concentrated in sectors such as defense, where decreases are desirable.

Nevertheless, production figures are far less sensitive to measurement problems than those in which the value of goods in rubles must be aggregated. One may question this or that precise figure on specific items in table 3-2, but there can be no argument about the overall picture presented. The level of production of almost any manufactured good, including a wide variety of consumer goods, has suffered a steady and dramatic decline since 1990. The decline of consumer goods production in 1994 and 1995 was especially steep.

In the long run the real problem was the decline in the production of capital goods. A drastic change in the structure of production is needed so that both the consumer and the producer receive more items that they want and need (for example, in agriculture, smaller tractors instead of the excessively large ones of the past). Russia needs new assembly lines and machine tools. Yet, machinery production has decreased 55 percent since 1990.

Falling production of agricultural machinery, fertilizer, and pesticides inevitably hampered agricultural production. In 1995 grain production was down 50

Table 3-2. Production of Selected Commodities, 1990–95

Commodity	1990	1991	1992	1993	1994	1995
Petroleum (million tons)	516	462	399	352	318	307
Coal (million tons)	395	353	337	305	272	262
Steel (million tons)	90	77	67	58	49	51
Tractors (thousands)	214	178	137	89	29	21
Excavators (thousands)	23	21	15	13	7	5
Mineral fertilizer (million tons)	16	15	12	9	8	9
Agricultural pesticides (thousand tons)	111	87	65	39	19	n.a.
Toilet soap (thousand tons)	190	151	114	82	56	n.a.
Timber (million cubic tons)	304	269	238	175	119	n.a.
Cement (million tons)	83	77	62	50	37	36
Cattle (millions of head)	57	55	52	49	49	39
Cattle excluding cows (millions of head)	37	34	32	29	29	22
Pigs (millions of head)	38	35	31	28	29	23
Grain (millions of tons)	116[a]	89	107	99	81	63
Cars (millions)	1.2	1.1	1.0	1.0	0.8	0.8
Paper (million tons)	5.2	4.8	3.6	2.9	2.2	2.8
Television (millions)	4.7	4.4	3.7	4.0	2.2	1.0
Refrigerators (millions)	3.7	3.7	3.2	3.5	2.7	1.7
Shoes (million pairs)	385	336	220	146	76	52
Cloth (billion square meters)	8.5	7.6	5.1	3.7	2.2	1.8
Socks, stockings (million pairs)	872	743	677	547	353	285

Sources: 1990–92 figures: *Rossiiskaia federatsiia v 1992 goda: Statisticheskii ezhegodnik* (Moscow: Respublikanskii informatsionno-izdatel'skii tsentr, 1993); 1993: *Ekonimika i zhizn*, no. 6 (February 1994), pp. 7–8; 1994: *Rossiiskii statisticheskii ezhegodnik. 1995* (Moscow: Goskomstat, 1995); 1995: FBIS, *Daily Report: Central Eurasia*, February 20, 1996, supplement.

n.a. Not available.

a. The average for 1976–80 was 106 million tons; for 1981–85 it was 99 million tons; and for 1986–90 it was 114 million tons. *Narodnoe khoziaistvo RSFSR v 1990 g.* (Moscow: Goskomstat, 1990), p. 420.

percent from 1990. This situation was the result of the low prices paid for agricultural products and the inability of collective farms and private farmers to purchase needed inputs.

As the economy faltered and production continued to fall while the income of a few soared, it was inevitable that someone would have to bear the cost. To a considerable extent, additional pressure was put on the same groups that were

**Table 3-3. Income from Basic Job, by Gender and Age,
Month before Election, 1993, 1995**

Rubles unless otherwise specified

Year	Men	Women	Men only 18–24	25–34	35–44	45–54	55–64
1993	89,300	59,700	77,900	102,000	88,200	91,000	68,700
1995	637,400	367,700	805,800	671,100	691,300	591,200	363,800
Percent change	710	620	1,030	660	780	680	530

Sources: See table 1-2. Excludes those working while on pension or studying.

already suffering disproportionately in 1993—middle-aged and older men, people over age 50, and women. Discrimination against women was not limited those employed in low-skill jobs: male professionals earned 717,000 rubles a month, compared with 388,000 for women; male skilled workers earned 625,355 rubles and women 373,000. As table 3-4 shows, persons older than 50 marginally increased their employment rates from 1993 to 1995, but as table 3-3 shows, they did so by accepting very low paying jobs.

Table 3-3 implies the need for deepest reflection about the way economic reform is usually interpreted in the West. The services sector was mostly privatized by 1995, it was said to constitute a larger percentage of the Russian economy than before, and private salaries were often said to be higher than those in the state sector. Because women had traditionally made up a large part of service workers, the logical conclusion was that women's wages should be improving.

In fact, the services sector did not grow significantly. The percentage of persons employed in industry declined from 35.7 percent to 30.1 percent, and the percentage employed in agriculture increased from 10.7 percent to 14.5 percent as those who could not survive in the city returned to the countryside. The share employed in trade and public eating establishments declined from 7.2 percent to 5.4 percent.[8]

The service sector includes high-paid banking positions and very low-paid jobs selling goods on the street. Those with a rosy view of Russian economic reform have pointed to the high-paid positions visible to foreigners in Moscow and St. Petersburg and have been silent about the lower-paid jobs and the virtual disappearance of services such as dry cleaning because people cannot afford them. It was as if the sale of apples by unemployed industrial workers in the American depression of the 1930s were praised as a positive development because it increased the size of service sector.

The continuing drop in production between 1993 and 1995 began to be translated into a major drop in the level of employment. The continued semi-employment of people at their former place of work makes measuring the level of unemployment difficult. In our survey, we adopted the most minimal measurement method by asking people if they were employed and then asking the reason if the answer was no. This methodology produced unemployment figures of 3.3 percent and 5.8 percent of all adults for 1993 and 1995, respectively. If those older than age 60 are excluded, the figures rise to 4.1 percent and 7.2 percent.

A more accurate picture emerges from table 3-4 on the percentage of people actually employed. Retirement begins at 55 for women and 60 for men, and employment rates above those ages were always low. By 1995 the employment rates of men of men younger than 55 and women younger than 50 were also seriously affected by the depression. The proportion of respondents who were employed fell from 70 percent in 1993 to 63 percent in 1995. Only 46 percent held full-time jobs; 26 percent reported they had rarely been paid on time during the previous six months, and 15 percent said they had not been paid at all. A total of 25 percent of adults held full-time jobs and usually or always received their paycheck on time.

From a political point of view, the differences in employment that occurred in cities of different sizes is even more important (table 3-5). Since the beginning Yeltsin had discriminated against villages and smaller towns and subsidized the larger cities. By 1995 production had fallen to such levels that the urban subsidies had to be financed at the expense of a much broader proportion of the population than in 1993. By 1995 virtually all cities of fewer than 1 million people had begun to feel the sting of government policy.

Not surprisingly, the population as a whole certainly had no sense of a turnaround in conditions in December 1995. In 1993 they had seen a serious deterioration in their position in the previous year, and their view was virtually identical two years later. In answer to the question, "How has your family economic and family situation changed in the last year?" the response was:

	1993	1995
Improved a lot	3%	3%
Improved a little	13	13
Remained unchanged	24	21
Worsened a little	23	24
Worsened a lot	34	37
Difficult to say	3	2

Table 3-4. Respondents Who Were Employed, by Age and Gender, 1993, 1995

Percent

	Total		Men		Women	
Age	1993	1995	1993	1995	1993	1995
65–69	24	13	34	18	21	11
60–64	25	20	37	27	18	15
55–59	54	49	77	71	41	32
50–54	81	76	86	77	75	75
45–49	92	84	94	86	90	83
35–44	92	82	94	84	90	81
25–34	83	79	91	86	75	71
Younger than 25	63	54	71	63	54	45

Sources: Includes those working while on pension or studying.

Only in cities with more than 1 million people did the number of those who thought their family's economic conditions was improving or unchanged (48.0 percent) equal the number who thought they were getting worse (48.1 percent). In towns with less than 10,000 people, 34 percent thought the family position was improving or unchanged; 41 percent of those living in cities with populations between 100,000 and 1 million thought it was improving.

Table 3-5. Employment and Income, by Population of Place of Residence, 1993, 1995

Percent unless otherwise specified

Population of place of residence	Employed		Usually paid on time 1995	Family income (rubles)		Percent change 1993–95
	1993	1995		1993	1995	
Less than 10,000	62	56	37	79,000	541,000	680
10,000–99,999	64	58	44	118,000	879,000	680
100,000–499,999	70	59	55	133,000	764,000	570
500,000–999,999	76	58	55	149,000	916,000	610
1,000,000–1,999,999	71	61	63	143,000	853,000	600
Moscow and St. Petersburg	62	65	84	132,000	1,090,000	830
Small fishing and mining towns	82	74	44	335,000	1,600,000	480

Sources: See table 1-2. Those who refused to report an income and those in the top 1 percent of the income distribution were excluded.

Views about the coming year were different only in that many were uncertain: 2 percent believed conditions would improve a lot and 10 percent a little; 20 percent thought they would remain the same. Twenty-six percent believed conditions would get worse, and 42 percent said it was difficult to answer.

When asked, "on whom, in your opinion, does an improvement of your life primarily now depend?" only 24 percent answered "yourself," while 56 percent pointed to the government or one of its branches. Without question, they think that the government is not doing a satisfactory job. Less than 10 percent believed that "things in Russia [are] going in a correct . . . direction" and 66 percent in an incorrect one. As one can well imagine, all this had a major impact on attitudes on a broad range of questions, on evaluation of Boris Yeltsin and opposition parties, and on their voting behavior in the 1995 election.

4

The 1995 Duma Election

The 1995 parliamentary election was held under very different circumstances than the one in 1993. The sense of crisis that had pervaded the earlier campaign had largely vanished. Although unsure of the election's outcome, Russians were certain that a Duma would emerge after December 17 and that it would be seated in parliament's headquarters in January. Moreover, while the voters in 1993 had a very limited choice in the left-center and moderate nationalist segments of the spectrum, the 1995 ballot included many more credible alternatives. Indeed, forty-three parties were on the ballot.

Russian public opinion had also evolved in the intervening two years. At the time of the 1993 Duma election, the Russian public was already in an unhappy mood, and their dissatisfaction had only deepened by December 1995. The approval rating of Boris Yeltsin summarized the situation dramatically.

Do you approve the activity of B. N. Yeltsin in the post of president of Russia?

	1993	1995
Completely approve	11%	3%
Approve on the whole	24	13
Disapprove on the whole	26	29
Completely disapprove	27	44
Difficult to answer	11	11

In the December 1995 election, only four of the forty-three parties on the ballot reached the 5 percent threshold required to achieve seats in the Duma. Some who looked at the vote won by these four parties noted that the 11.2 percent of the vote received by the Liberal Democrats and the 22.3 by the Communists in 1995 totaled two points less than the 35.3 percent the two received together in 1993. Similarly, the 10.1 percent of Our Home Is Russia,

6.9 percent of Yabloko, and 3.9 percent of Gaidar's Russia's Democratic Choice was only three points less than the 23.4 percent total won by Russia's Choice and Yabloko in 1993. Those who emphasized these facts argued that little had changed in the political landscape.

This analysis, however, represented little more than political spin. The four parties who received seats in the Duma in 1995 gathered only 50 percent of the total vote cast for the forty-three parties on the ballot. Any realistic understanding of voting behavior in 1995 must take the other 50 percent into account. When that is done, it is clear that a major shift of voting behavior toward the conservatives had occurred. It reflected a major shift in public opinion.

The Sources of Popular Dissatisfaction

There were a number of sources of public dissatisfaction at the end of the 1995. Foremost, of course, was the state of the economy and the policies people think have contributed to it. In 1993 only 13 percent of all respondents favored a rapid transition to a market economy; in 1995 the percentage was even lower:

What do you think about the transition to a market economy in Russia?

	1993	1995
The transition should be rapid	13%	7%
The transition should be gradual	42	44
I am against a market economy	19	23
Difficult to answer	25	27

A second source of grievance is a growing popular discontent with the breakup of the Soviet Union.

How do you assess the disintegration of the Soviet Union?

	1993	1995
It was a useful thing	10%	5%
It was more useful than harmful	10	9
It was more harmful than useful	18	20
It was harmful	51	56
Difficult to answer	11	10

The explosive aspect of these two sets of attitudes for both Russia and the West is that Russians see a link between the two. When asked whether you "think the West is pursuing the goal of weakening Russia with its economic advice," a 2-to-1 majority among those with an opinion answered affirmatively in 1993. This ratio was 3 to 1 in 1995.

Do you think the West is pursuing the goal of weakening
Russia with its economic advice?

	1993	1995
Yes, you are sure of it	28%	36%
You are not sure, but probably yes	24	24
You are not sure, but probably no	14	13
You are sure that it is not	11	7
Difficult to answer	23	21

Russians also see a link between the rapidity of economic reform and a third grievance—the pervasiveness of crime and lawlessness. In January 1996 Jeffrey Sachs, the Harvard economist who was the most prominent spokesman for shock therapy and was an adviser to the Gaidar government, wrote that the high level of corruption in Russia was unprecedented.[1] They sometimes refer to privatization (*privatizatsiia*) as *prikhvatizatsiia,* or *grabification.*[2]

When Russians were asked to pick the most important feature of democracy, 50 percent of those with an opinion chose legality and law and order as against 19 percent each who selected people's power and individual freedom and 6 percent who listed private property.[3] The concern about increasing crime and disorder focuses on what is seen as economic crime: the penetration of private business by the Mafia, insider privatization, speculation, government corruption, and so forth. As they are used in Russia, *Mafia* and *successful businessmen* are often difficult to distinguish.

Our Russian colleagues included a question on the 1995 survey that we considered too vague to be useful: "Do you think there exist definite forces who are guilty for all the misfortunes of our country?" The answers are, in fact, too diffuse to reveal whom the Russian people really suspect, but they do document the depth of the suspicion.

Completely agree	45%
Generally agree	20
Generally disagree	7
Completely disagree	8
Difficult to answer	20

Economic Reform

The question about whether the transition to a market economy is proceeding too quickly serves surprisingly well to summarize the attitudes on a broad range of questions about economic reform. It therefore allows us to illustrate the differences in attitudes of different groups. For example, 4 percent of those without a high school degree favor rapid economic reform, compared with 7 percent of those with a high school diploma and 12 percent of college graduates. Only 2 percent of those age 55 or older but 14 percent of those between 18 and 24 favor rapid reform. Rapid reform is approved by 11 percent of managers and 9 percent of professionals but just 4 percent of workers and white-collar personnel without a college degree. Eight percent of men favor rapid reform compared with 5 percent of women. Similar differences are found when more specific questions are asked about economic reform.

People, of course, vary in their attitudes toward various aspects of reform. A general question about privatization shows that people do not perceive it as a yes or no question but spread their answers across a range of options.

What do you think about the process of privatization of state property in Russia?

	1993	1995
Privatization should be accelerated	17%	5%
Privatization should be continued at the same pace	18	11
Privatization should be slowed down	8	10
Privatization should be stopped	13	21
Privatization should be reversed	10	17
Difficult to answer	34	36

Opinion also varies greatly on types of privatization. Only 7 percent wholly approve the privatization of big enterprises, but 25 percent completely support the privatization of housing (down, to be sure, from 40 percent in 1993), and 28 percent generally support it. In 1995 we did not repeat a 1993 question about support for privatization of trade because our Russian colleagues insisted it would show 100 percent support and that other questions would be more useful. They no doubt exaggerated, but they surely were right in predicting that support would have been even greater than for privatization of housing.

But as the reactions to questions on acceleration of privatization and privatization of big enterprises illustrate, various questions show the very limited support the population holds for any radical reform. Only 12 percent think people should be free to buy and sell land without restrictions; 9 percent would give farms and stores the right to sell their produce at market prices; 9 percent completely support foreign investment; and 12 percent are opposed to tariffs. Only 4 percent believe "Russia should as quickly as possible use the experience of the West."

But by the same token, only a small minority are opposed to all economic reform: the 15 percent who oppose privatization of housing, the 17 percent who would reverse all privatization, and the 19 percent who are completely opposed to foreign investment. But, again, opinions vary with the type of step described. Thirty-five percent are completely opposed to the privatization of big enterprises, 40 percent are against all sale and purchase of land, and 61 percent would retain strict controls on food prices as opposed to 26 percent who favor the middle option, regulation of prices but not strict controls.

Perhaps the most interesting difference in attitudes is one that did not occur. One of the most frequent arguments for privatization, and especially voucher-based privatization, was that it would build mass political support for economic reform. That managers support economic reform no doubt does reflect their hope that they can gain control of property. Even if Zyugonov wins the presidency, *nomenklatura* privatization has been so widespread that it is hard to imagine he will want to end the principle of privatization, especially the elite apartments the Communists have privatized.

But hopes about the mass consequences of privatization for support of economic reform have not been realized. Sixty-two percent of the respondents owned some kind of shares in enterprises or mutual funds, and 35 percent of those in the cities larger than 500,000 own their apartments. (In the villages and smaller towns, a large number have always owned their own houses.)

The 7 percent of respondents who report working in private enterprises are stronger supporters of economic reform, but it makes little difference among the others whether they work in state enterprises or those based on stock ownership. Personal ownership of equity shares or a privatized apartment is not associated with any significant difference in views on economic reform. Besides, although 8 percent of respondents reported owning shares in active mutual funds, 13 percent said they owned shares in dishonest, failed ones. The attitudes of the losers should not be difficult to imagine. The following table shows opinions about the privatization of big enterprises, but the distribution of responses could be matched on other questions as well.

Do you support privatization of big enterprises?

Ownership status	Complete support	Support on whole	Don't support on whole	Completely oppose	Difficult to answer
No shares	6.6%	14.3%	18.7%	38.9%	21.2%
Shares in own enterprise	6.6	11.1	18.5	44.0	19.5
Shares in mutual fund	8.9	19.6	18.1	31.6	21.8
Shares in failed mutual fund	4.9	15.1	21.1	41.0	17.0
A privatized apartment	6.7	15.4	17.5	36.7	23.5
Total population	6.6%	13.6%	17.7%	35.0%	26.5%

The Former Soviet Union

People's attitudes toward the former Soviet Union are also highly complex. The case for an independent Russia was, in fact, made in the fall of 1991 on economic grounds. The price of the union, it was said, was continued subsidies for other republics; an independent Russia unencumbered by them would be economically much more successful. Radical economic reformers such as Yegor Gaidar strongly opposed steps toward economic integration—even voluntary economic integration—of Russia with Ukraine or Belarus, and they still do.

It is this economic argument that Russians are rejecting by a huge majority when they say the breakup of the Soviet Union was harmful. And it is this argument that contributes mightily to their strong suspicion that the radical economic reformers were agents of U.S. foreign policy in a treasonable sense. Russians also resent the complaints in the non-Russian republics about a Russian empire that benefited only Russians (Russians think there was a Moscow empire that suppressed Russian and non-Russian regions equally). This resentment, as well as guilt about the Russians abandoned in "the Near Abroad"—the former republics of the Soviet Union—lead to a belief that the latter should be supported.

Should the Russian government defend the rights of Russians living in the former republics of the USSR?

	1993	1995
Yes, it should	92%	90%
No, it should not	2	3
Difficult to answer	5	7

Russians also continue to have a very difficult time thinking of former republics, especially Ukraine, as independent countries. Because Russians strongly favor tariffs on industrial and agricultural goods (62 percent in favor, 12 percent against, and 25 percent uncertain), they should favor tariffs on Ukrainian goods imported into Russia if Ukraine were thought of as a foreign country. But only 6 percent choose this option.

What in your opinion should be the relationship between Russia and Ukraine?

Ukraine should be an independent state with strict customs controls on its border with Russia	6%
Ukraine should be an independent state with open borders with Russia	25
Ukraine and Russia should be united into a confederative state	13
Ukraine and Russia should be united into a single state	40
Difficult to answer	15

Most striking of all is the decreasing number of inhabitants of Russia who identify with Russia as their motherland (*rodina*). In the past most would have stated that "the Soviet Union" was their motherland, but in 1993 only 29 percent agreed; 50 percent chose Russia and 12 percent the republic or region in which they lived. It seemed likely that a permanent change in national identification was under way. But in 1995 only 39 percent of the respondents answered Russia, while the number listing the Soviet Union rose to 39 percent and those identifying with their region to 23 percent. Among the ethnic Russians alone, those who chose Russia dwindled from 55 percent to 41 percent.

Older Russians are more inclined than younger ones to consider the Soviet Union their motherland. Yet it is striking how much Russians of all ages have drifted away from identification with Russia, the older generation toward the Soviet Union or their local region, the younger primarily to their region.

What do you consider to be your motherland?
(ethnic Russians only)

	Russia		USSR		Region		Don't know	
Age	1993	1995	1993	1995	1993	1995	1993	1995
Over 65	53%	33%	33%	45%	8%	19%	6%	3%
55–64	61	36	25	39	11	19	3	5
45–54	50	45	37	39	11	18	2	3
35–44	53	40	30	34	13	20	5	5
25–34	54	45	27	24	14	24	5	7
Under 25	57	50	24	22	17	25	3	4

What is, however, difficult to judge is the political meaning of these feelings, other than to reenforce hostility toward Boris Yeltsin as the man who broke up the Soviet Union nine months after three-quarters of the population voted in a free referendum to maintain it. Certainly the Russian people do not seem chauvinists determined to reunite the union at all costs and restore the old domination. When asked to choose whether they would support a leader who would give priority to the reestablishment of the Soviet Union or to a Russia developing within its borders, 30 percent favored reestablishment, 46 percent favored Russia, and 23 percent were not sure. Forty-five percent—only marginally less than in 1993—believe Russians in the republics inside Russia should learn the local language, while 39 percent disagree. They must believe this even more strongly in the case of the former union republics.

The attitudes toward Chechnia are particularly interesting: only 39 percent would insist on its inclusion into Russia; 39 percent would give it independence. Most striking of all, respondents' attitudes about Chechnia were virtually irrelevant to their voting behavior in the Duma election. The opinions of Zhirinovsky and Gaidar about the breakup of the former Soviet Union seemed polar opposites, but 38 percent of the Zhirinovsky voters and 39 percent of the Gaidar voters supported Chechen independence. The Communist and Agrarian voters likewise gave 39 percent support to Chechen independence, while General Lebed's supporters were only marginally less certain at 36 percent. Those voting for Viktor Chernomyrdin's Our Home Is Russia are more supportive of the government's effort to preserve Russian territorial integrity, but even 33 percent of them supported Chechnia's independence.

It is crucial to understand these attitudes. When the Communist-dominated Duma passes a nonbinding resolution annulling the dissolution of the Soviet Union, but Zyuganov damns the war in Chechnia as an unacceptable civil war, some in the West think Zyuganov has a secret plan to reunite the country, probably by force. Whatever his intentions, his symbolic support for the Soviet Union on the fifth anniversary of the referendum on its breakup, his promise of greater economic integration, and his denunciation of the government for taking steps to retain Chechnia by force are precisely the stances that should be taken by a Russian politician who reads the polls and tries to appeal to public opinion.

The Competing Parties

The 1993 electoral law was retained in its essentials in 1995, with half the deputies elected by proportional representation and half in single-member districts. Because they had two years to prepare for the Duma election, Russian politicians had ample time to form coalitions and to build party organizations in the provinces. Yet only the Communists achieved a solid party organization outside Moscow, and, with forty-three parties on the ballot, efforts at building coalitions were mostly unsuccessful. If one is to understand the evolution in Russian voting behavior between 1993 and 1995, the parties have to be discussed as groups—no easy task. In Russia, *reform* became the word for *revolution* and *democrats* the word for supporters of an authoritarian presidency. Politicians at the other end of the political spectrum tried to appropriate the term *patriots* for themselves, implying and often saying directly that their opponents served the interests of Russia's long-time foreign enemy. The traditional distinction between liberals and conservatives was utterly confusing in a context in which supporters of Margaret Thatcher were the radical transformers and Communists were the conservatives.

In the past few years, Russian political commentators have begun to move toward western nomenclature by using the terms *Left* and *Right* in their western meanings. The Communists and those close to them are the Left (or, pejoratively, the Reds), while the strong pro-market forces are the Right. As in the West, the strongly nationalist Right does not fit easily in this spectrum, for these parties are usually more pro-market than the Communists but still have a strong element of economic populism.[4] Nevertheless, because these labels begin to put Russia in a meaningful comparative context, we will use them in this book.

The Right-Wing Parties

In 1993 there was no doubt that Gaidar's Russia's Choice was the major rightist party on the ballot. In 1995 Gaidar again ran with this party, although now it was called Russia's Democratic Choice. Gaidar positioned himself to the right of the government on economic reform and also sharply criticized Yeltsin for his military intervention in Chechenia. Other parties—Sergei Shakhrai's PRES, Boris Fedorov's Forward Russia, Common Cause, and the Party of Economic Freedom—propounded similar views.

After the 1993 elections Yeltsin and Chernomyrdin tried to distance themselves from the radical reformers who had run on the Russia's Choice ticket. Our Home Is Russia was established as what they called a center-right party, one espousing stability, order, and continuity. Our Home Is Russia included more officials of the central and regional executive branch than did any other party: 70 of the 209 candidates on its regional lists were regional officials in the executive branch, and Our Home Is Russia was called "the party of power."

Table 4-1. Attitudes toward Economic Reform among Those Intending to Vote, by Party, December 1995

Percent

Party	Oppose all economic reform	Permit private sale of big enterprises	Favor sale of land[a]	Against strict control of food prices	No limits on income of wealthy
Communist	48	7	31 (6)	22	10
Ryzhkov	30	6	29 (13)	9	8
Agrarian	31	11	28 (5)	33	23
Zhirinovsky	28	17	50 (16)	19	18
Skokov-Lebed	20	30	58 (7)	42	22
Yabloko	9	33	72 (15)	55	43
Chernomyrdin	8	40	66 (14)	53	32
Gaidar	8	43	78 (22)	69	66

Sources: See table 1-2.

a. Numbers in parentheses are percent of people who favor unrestricted sales.

Yet, however Our Home Is Russia tried to present itself, the party continued to support the tight money, privatization, and free-trade policies that had caused such discontent. As table 4-1 shows, on average the party's supporters had only marginally different views from those of Gaidar on economic reform and, as table 4-2 shows, their views were only somewhat more distant on nationalist issues. In our survey, more of Gaidar's 1993 voters decided in 1995 to vote for Our Home Is Russia than for Gaidar's party.

In addition, the name Our Home Is Russia had a significance not obvious to an American. Like the name of Gaidar's party, Russia's Democratic Choice, it deliberately associated the party with the creation of an independent Russia (*Rossiia*). It is not surprising, then, that most of Our Home Is Russia supporters were very much among the westernizers, but also not very surprising that the party did not pick up a large following among the majority of citizens who thought the breakup of the Soviet Union had been a mistake.

The final major party on the right was Yabloko, led by economist Grigory Yavlinsky. Because Yavlinsky is running for president, we will postpone most of our discussion of him to the next chapter. Suffice it to say, however, that although Yavlinsky called himself a centrist and vaguely advocated greater moderation, his policy positions were difficult to distinguish from Gaidar's.

Table 4-2.   Respondent Attitudes on Nationalism, by Party, 1995
Percent

Party	USSR breakup was useful	West does not intend to weaken Russia	Ukraine should be independent	Against foreign investment	Rodina is Russia	Make Chechenia independent
Communist	3	6	14	50	27	39
Ryzhkov	9	18	27	63	30	52
Agrarian	10	12	37	38	39	39
Zhirinovsky	11	10	32	41	36	38
Skokov-Lebed	13	7	38	29	52	36
Yabloko	27	38	44	16	53	41
Chernomyrdin	26	34	48	26	50	33
Gaidar	39	56	57	16	62	39

Sources: See table 1-2.

The Left-Wing Parties

The main victor in the 1995 parliamentary elections was the Communist Party of the Russian Federation, led by Gennady Zyuganov. It too will be discussed in the next chapter, but one thing should be emphasized here: the Communists not only won the most seats in the Duma, but also consolidated their position as the dominant alternative to Yeltsin on the left. This was no mean feat. Ivan Rybkin was attempting to create a Western social-democratic party—the Bloc of Ivan Rybkin—and had the status of chairman of the Duma to bolster his name recognition. Despite ample funding, he succeeded in obtaining only 1.1 percent of the vote. The Agrarian party had won 8 percent of the vote in 1993, but it fell to 3.8 percent in 1995. Former Soviet premier Nikolai Ryzhkov's new Power to the People party won only 1.6 percent of the vote. Indeed, the nationalist party that was most Peronist in its endorsement of social welfare measures—Aleksandr Rutskoi's Great Power (*Derzhava*)—also received only 2.6 percent of the vote, and Rutskoi quickly endorsed Zyuganov for president in 1996.

The only left-wing alternative to the Communists that gained some credibility was a bloc of more radical organizations, Communists–Working Russia–For the Soviet Union, led by Viktor Anpilov. Anpilov had been a leader of the demonstrators that had stormed the parliament building in October 1993, and he had been arrested for that action. He was forthright in his desire to return to the old

Soviet system and the old Soviet Union, and his bloc received 4.5 percent of the vote.

Yet, even Anpilov helped the Communists become the dominating party on the left. Zyuganov was trying to position himself more toward the political center, but the core of his support strongly opposed economic reform. As he made statements to appeal to this core, he risked frightening those toward the center whom he needed to help the party achieve a majority. Anpilov helped Zyuganov with the centrists by reminding them what a Bolshevik was really like.

The Nationalist Parties

A third major alternative to the current government is provided by the so-called nationalist parties. Unfortunately, the designation hides more than it reveals, for it has an inevitable ambiguity in contemporary Russia. Nationalism under the tsar and then under communism was associated with a large multiethnic state or empire that was a world power. Russian nationalism today can mean either a restoration of that state or a strong identification with the Russian part of it that seceded from the Soviet Union in 1991 under Yeltsin. Those who emphasize the present Russia (*Rossiia*) have given up half the country and have countenanced deindustrializing, especially the defense industry. They therefore find it difficult to appeal to traditional national themes.

It was the Communist party that always opposed the disintegration of the Soviet Union and that calls for its reintegration. The supporters of the Communist party are more nationalistic than those of the two nationalist parties (Zhirinovsky and Skokov-Lebed in table 4-2). The supporters of the other "communist" parties are similar in their opinions to suppporters of the nationalists. This similarity reflects the fact that all these parties are speaking in basically similar ways on national themes.

The main difference between the nationalist parties and the communist groups is the more moderate position of the nationalists on economic reform. Indeed, as chapter 5 shows, General Lebed can even claim—implausibly to be sure—to have the same platform as Yavlinsky. The parties' appeals are reflected in differences of those who support them. Only 8 percent of the supporters of the left-wing parties in table 4-1 favor privatization of big enterprises, compared with 25 percent of the nationalists and 39 percent of the right-wing supporters. Similarly, 32 percent of the supporters of the left-wing parties approve of free or restricted sale of land, but 55 percent of the nationalist supporters and 72 percent of the right-wingers approve.

Even taking this factor into account, most of the so-called nationalist parties are hard to distinguish from the communists. Nikolai Ryzhkov's party, Power to the People, had included Sergei Baburin, one of the parliament's most outspoken nationalists, in the number two spot on his list, but it was very close to the communists both in its program and the views of its voters. Ryzhkov's faction in the Duma, "People's Power," included a number of former Communist officials, and Ryzhkov himself has already endorsed Zyuganov for president. Stanislav Govorukhin, leader of a nationalist party with his name, has joined the Ryzhkov's faction. Aleksandr Rutskoi in 1990 had been one of the few deputies elected to the Central Committee of the Russian Communist party in 1990, and in 1991 he organized a reform Communist party. Boris Gromov of the Fatherland party had been vice presidential candidate of the Communist party in 1991.

Leaving aside Nikolai Lysenko's National Republican Party of Russia, which is fascist by any definition, the two nationalist parties that were clearly distinguished from the communists are the Liberal Democrats of Vladimir Zhirinovsky and the Congress of Russian Communities of Yury Skokov and Aleksandr Lebed. Both were to the right (pro-market) side of the communists on the economic spectrum, and both emphasize ethnic Russians rather than the multiethnic union. Because both will provide presidential contenders in 1996, they will be discussed in the next chapter.

The Centrist Parties

None of the parties that might be called centrist won enough votes to receive representation in the Duma, and it is difficult to know how they should be classified. None was ever considered a serious contender for power, although Women of Russia had been expected to reach the 5 percent minimum. They encompassed a range of platforms, and there is little reason to discuss them in any detail because most will prove ephemeral.

Indeed, even in 1995 it is not clear if voters saw much connection between platform and message. The leaders of the Women's party, whose platform was essentially social-democratic, moved closer to a pro-Yeltsin position, and this was one reason it did so poorly in the election. The potentially more interesting party—that of Svyatoslav Fedorov, a famous 69-year-old eye surgeon who has a network of private eye-surgery clinics around the country—was the Workers' Self-Management party. Its platform seemed leftist, and Fedorov himself joined Nikolai Ryzhkov's semicommunist faction in the Duma. Yet Fedorov's supporters were moderate and considered him, whatever his rhetoric, as a business-man who would favor economic reform. By contrast, the politician whose name was first in the title of the party Pamfilova-Gurov-Vladimir Lysenko had been closely associated with Yeltsin and joined a faction primarily composed of radicals. Yet the supporters of the party were leftist. Cedar, the green party, generally appealed to pro-Western reformers, but environmental parties are always ambivalent at best toward the free operation of the market. The Indus-trialists and Trade Unions party was dominated by the industrialists and there-fore was more favorable to *nomenklatura* privatization than most of its voters.

Rather than try to sort out these inconsistencies, we need to make only one important point. Some 14.5 percent of the population voted for these parties and another 4.4 percent voted for the 20 minor parties we find difficult to classify. It is unclear what they will do in the first round of the presidential election if the choice is narrow, and it is crucial what they will do on the second round when they will be forced to make a choice.

The Election Results

The results of the 1995 Duma elections can be described in many ways. Most analysts have concentrated on the major parties, but the four parties that achieved the 5 percent minimum needed to obtain seats in the Duma received only 50 percent of the vote. If we are to use the Duma election results to anticipate presidential election patterns, we must look at the other parties as well.

This is not a simple task. Some of the forty-three parties are so obscure that it is difficult to know what they stood for, let alone what the public thought they stood for. In general, however, their vote is too insignificant to matter. But in other cases, decisions on classification can affect interpretations. A number of parties that were considered nationalist—those of Nikolai Ryzhkov, Aleksandr Rutskoi, and Stanislav Govorukhin—in many ways seemed closer to leftist parties. Ryzhkov and Rutskoi soon supported Zyuganov for president and will be classified as leftist here.

Svyatoslav Fedorov's Workers' Self-Management party and the parties of Pamfilov and Gurov will be classified as centrist. They could be classified as rightist parties, but for the purposes of this book, it seems likely that many of their supporters will vote for Zyuganov.[5]

Whatever the precise classification of minor parties, the general picture of the election results is clear. First, as table 4-3 shows, the strong leftist and nationalist

Table 4-3. Share of Votes, by Ideological Party Types, 1993, 1995[a]

Ideology	Percent 1993	Percent 1995	Total votes 1993	Total votes 1995
Left-wing	20.4	35.5	10,958,920	24,078,000
Nationalist	22.9	18.3	12,318,562	12,428,000
Right-wing (reform)	34.2	24.5	18,374,104	16,601,000
Centrist	16.3	14.5	6,784,433	9,860,000
Miscellaneous	1.9	4.4	1,047,714	2,999,000
Against all	4.2	2.8	2,267,973	1,918,000
Total	100	100	53,751,696	67,994,200

Sources: See chap. 4, notes 6 and 7.

a. "Left-wing" includes the Communist and Agrarian parties in 1993 and in addition the parties of Anpilov, Rutskoi, and Nikolai Ryzhkov in 1995. "Nationalist" includes the Liberal Democrats in 1993 and in addition the parties of Lebed, Govorukhin, My Fatherland, For the Motherland, and the National-Republicans in 1995. "Right-wing" includes Russia's Democratic Choice, Yabloko, PRES, and RDDR in 1993 and in addition Our Home Is Russia, Boris Fedorov's Forward Russia, and Our Common Cause in 1995.

opposition parties increased their share of the party list vote from 43 percent in 1993 to 54 percent in 1995.

The right-wing or reform parties' share shrank from 34 percent to 24.5 percent, and even these figures understate the diminishing support for radical politicians. In 1993 Gaidar's Russia's Choice was unquestionably radical, while PRES was headed by two highly radical deputy premiers in the government. Russia's Choice and PRES combined received 22.2 percent of the vote in 1993; if Yabloko and Our Home Is Russia are considered only semiradical, as Yabloko and the Russian Democratic Reform party (RDDR) were in 1993, the four radical parties on the ballot received only 7.9 percent of the vote in 1995.

It is not enough to speak only of change in percentage of party vote. In 1993, about 57.7 million persons voted in the referendum on the constitution, and 56.4 million cast valid votes. Only 53.8 million valid votes are reported to have been cast in the party list vote, perhaps because of confusion over different voting methods used in the two elections.[6] In 1995 the combination of much higher turnout and greater voter familiarity with the new type of ballot resulted in 67.9 million valid ballots being cast—an increase of 30 percent. As a result, a larger number of actual votes lay behind each percentage point of support received by each party. Thus simply to say that the communists increased their proportion of the vote from 12.4 percent to 22.4 percent masks the size of their gain. It is more relevant to say that support of the communists increased from 6.7 million to 14.4 million votes; support of the left-wing opposition parties as a whole increased from 11.0 million to 24.1 million.[7]

In addition to the party list vote, there were also elections in 225 districts throughout Russia. In 83 a candidate associated with one of the four major parties won. In 65 the winners were candidates of parties that did•not cross the 5 percent threshold, and 77 winners were independents. The 142 deputies that were not candidates from the four major parties could either join the faction of one of them or they could form new factions (to form a new faction, 23 deputies must agree).

The far right column of table 4-4 was calculated by subtracting the number of deputies earned by party in the party list vote from the total size of the faction that was formed in the early days of the new Duma. It provides a generally accurate view of the political leanings of the persons elected in the single-member districts, although there are some problems of analysis with the new factions and the independents.

The makeup of factions on the Left was fairly straightforward: the Agrarians came from the countryside and had always been closely allied to the communists. People's Power was formed by Nikolai Ryzhkov and deputies of similar persuasion. Russian Regions, however, was a strange mixture: it contained the leading proponent of a centralized Russia without republics (Sergei Shakhrai) and the leading defender of the republics (Ramazan Abdulatipov), the most radical populist of the Gorbachev era (Telman Gdlian) and the last commander in Afghanistan (Boris Gromov). On balance, Shakhrai and Gdlian seemed closer to the average outlook in the faction, but eight of the nine deputies elected as representing Gaidar's Russia's Democratic Choice refused to join Russian Regions or any other faction. Thus most independents were right-wing. They compensate for the conservatives and moderates in Russian Regions and make the totals of table 4-4 seem basically accurate.[8]

In any case, the basic fact suggested by table 4-4 is unchallengeable. The Left obtained 44 percent of the party list seats—but partly because one-half of the voters supported parties that did not reach the 5 percent minimum and had their votes redistributed. In the district elections the Left won a clear majority (54 percent) of the seats. Because there was no runoff, this did not mean the Left won 54 percent of the district vote (we do not have data on the ideological distribution of voters in district elections). But at a minimum, the great success of the Left in the districts is testimony to its superior political and organizational skills.

There are many ways to analyze the reasons for the increase in the vote of the leftist and nationalist opposition parties in 1995. The simplest may well be the

Table 4-4. Members of Duma Factions, by Election in Districts or Party List, 1995

Faction	Total in faction	Elected by party list	Elected in districts
Left-wing	221	99	122
Communists	149	99	50
People's Power	37	0	37
Agrarian	35	0	35
Nationalist	51	50	1
Liberal Democrats	51	50	1
Right-wing	152	76	76
Our Home Is Russia	65	45	20
Russian Regions	41	0	41
Yabloko	46	31	15
Independent	26	0	26

Sources: See table 1-2.

best. The country is in the midst of a major depression; 16 percent of the people think their economic position improved in the past year and 61 percent think it worsened; only 10 percent thinks the country is on the right course. One does not need sophisticated political science to explain why parties supporting government policy received 25 percent of the vote and strongly antigovernment parties 54 percent.

But with the opposition divided and a presidential election imminent in which one person must emerge victorious, it is important to try to get a deeper sense of the parties' demographic and socioeconomic sources of support. Even though our survey was conducted before the election, the results shown in table 4-5 generally corresponded to those actually reported.

We do not have space for a detailed analysis of table 4-5, but several points deserve emphasis. First, the pronounced difference in income or views on economic reform between men and women was not reflected in voting behavior. Half of the Women of Russia answers have been excluded in the gender entries (and only there), but even then women are marginally more centrist than men. It is likely that most Anpilov voters, few of whom are represented in our sample, were men, and this would increase the gender difference.

Table 4-5. Support for Party Types, by Respondent Socioeconomic Characteristic, 1993, 1995

Percent

Characteristic	Right-wing		Left-wing (minus Anpilov)		Nationalist		Other	
	1993	1995	1993	1995	1993	1995	1993	1995
Gender								
Male	37	25	20	35	24	23	19	17
Female	42	26	15	33	14	14	30	28
Age								
65 or older	39	16	28	52	8	11	24	21
55–64	41	18	23	42	17	16	20	25
45–54	33	20	17	33	23	18	26	29
35–44	40	30	14	30	22	17	25	24
25–34	43	34	12	21	18	18	27	27
18–24	43	28	9	8	25	27	24	37
Education								
Elementary	33	13	29	48	25	15	13	25
Incomplete secondary	30	16	23	41	23	20	25	24
Secondary diploma	36	27	15	27	24	20	26	26
Special secondary	41	29	12	26	19	15	29	30
Higher education	57	35	15	24	6	14	22	27
Occupation								
Manager	47	28	15	33	14	16	24	23
Professional	50	38	15	20	10	14	25	28
White collar	44	30	12	30	18	13	26	27
Worker	32	22	12	30	30	22	25	26
Collective farmer	12	15	43	51	17	18	28	16

Sources: See table 1-2.

Second, the decrease in support for the right-wing parties is reasonably consistent across the board, but it is particularly high in the core of reform support—people in the professions and management who have the most education. This group has shifted more to a centrist position. The strongest increase in support for the Left was among those older than age 55 and those without a high school diploma. A geographical cleavage has also been crucial in Russian politics. In all elections since 1989 the south has voted more conservatively than

Table 4-6. Vote in North and South, 1993, 1995

Percent

Region	Right-wing parties 1993	Right-wing parties 1995	Communist party (Zyuganov) 1993	Communist party (Zyuganov) 1995	All Left parties 1993	All Left parties 1995	Liberal Democrats 1993	Liberal Democrats 1995	Nationalists 1993	Nationalists 1995
Oblasts and republics of European Russia										
North	38	49	9	19	15	29	22	11	22	20
South	47	59	15	27	24	39	23	12	23	20
Oblasts (but not republics) of European Russia										
North	38	47	8	18	15	27	23	9	23	20
South	51	64	15	39	24	41	27	13	27	23
Oblasts (but not republics) of Asiatic Russia										
Total	39	54	9	22	15	32	23	15	23	22

Sources: See table 1-2.

the north, and this pattern continued in 1995. Indeed, as table 4-6 indicates, the difference between north and south on voting for the Communist and leftist parties was somewhat greater in 1995 than in 1993 in the European oblasts in which the analysis is usually concentrated. But the big story of the election was the change in voters' choices in the Urals section of European Russia and in Asiatic Siberia.[9]

In addition, the larger cities have always voted for more radical reformers than smaller cities and the countryside. This pattern was repeated in 1995 (table 4-7). But if the left-wing and nationalist vote is added, the smaller towns and villages became only marginally more oppositional in 1995 than in 1993, a difference that would have been more substantial if the Anpilov vote were included in 1995. The main difference is that in the countryside and small towns large numbers who voted for Zhirinovsky in 1993 supported a left-wing party in 1995.

A cursory comparison of the 1993 and 1995 support for communists and strong opposition parties in general gives the impression that they gained evenly in the north and south, in large cities and small. The opposition is still a distinct minority in the cities with populations of more than 1 million. This impression is accurate enough for general purposes, but its significance should not be overestimated.

In 1990 and 1993, cultural, psychological, and ideological factors were decisive elements in the election. The bulk of the population in the north and in larger cities—and not only the largest—thought of the Communist party as the

Table 4-7. Support for Political Party Types, by Population of Respondent's Place of Residence, 1993, 1995

Percent

Size of population	Right-wing 1993	Right-wing 1995	Left-wing 1993	Left-wing 1995	Nationalist 1993	Nationalist 1995
Less than 10,000	25	20	29	44	22	15
10,000–99,999	38	20	19	28	18	19
100,000–499,999	40	22	12	31	19	19
500,000–999,999	45	28	12	32	22	12
1,000,000–1,999,999	61	38	9	19	9	13
Moscow and St. Petersburg	62	42	9	16	11	12
Fishing and mining communities	33	25	10	20	37	13

Sources: See table 1-2.

symbol of the old system, political as much as economic. They considered "democrats," as they called themselves, the representatives of modernization and opportunity. Urban dwellers who might suffer most at first from the reduction of defense expenditures, the downsizing of industry, and exposure to foreign competition reassured themselves that, like the suffering in war, this was a necessary price to pay for an important good. Even the strong vote for Zhirinovsky in 1993 was as much a rejection of the Communist party as of the government.

Now the Communist party is far more trusted than Zhirinovsky and is the clear leader among the strongly oppositional parties. There is no evidence that people in the larger cities have given up on the market and democracy, but by the end of 1995 a great many had abandoned Yeltsin and turned against the program of radical economic reform his government had promoted. They were beginning to look at the Communist party not simply as a symbol of the best means to achieve their goals, but as a party that had an alternative program of economic reform.

This is of the utmost importance. In 1993 the Communists seemed a party limited in its appeal by a well-defined distrust. By 1995 they were clearly moving toward respectability among large segments of the population. This respectability has created the possibility of additional growth.

5

The Presidential Election:
The Candidates and Their Programs

Americans are used to presidential campaigns in which candidates are rather vague about their program, and "campaign oratory" has a thoroughly pejorative meaning. Yet the major American candidates are nominated by stable political parties, and they function within established institutions. They normally have a proven record. For the sophisticated observer, the surprises about American presidents come more from the mistakes they make—or the unexpected qualities they show—instead of from some drastic deviation from their past promises or record.

The situation in Russia is fundamentally different. *Time* magazine reports that Russians consider Yeltsin the "best guarantee of Russian democracy" but strongly suspect he will call off the June election.[1] No one would be willing to say flatly that as president, Zyuganov or Lebed would permit a new free election four years hence. The economic programs the candidates would enact are even more difficult to predict. One can plausibly hypothesize that Zyuganov would either pursue the kind of social-democratic programs followed by communist presidents in Poland and Hungary or that he would reintroduce large portions of the old communist system.

Moreover, although the Russian election is scheduled for June 16, 1996, it will differ from an American presidential election in important ways. First, there will be a runoff election, presumably on July 7, if no candidate receives a majority of the vote.[2] Second, a candidate can gain access to the ballot with only 1 million signatures (but no more than 70,000 in any one region). The government will provide a total of 4 billion rubles in campaign funds divided equally among the candidates and ten minutes of free time on each of three state television networks for any candidate who achieves the requisite number of signatures. Third, a candidate can drop off the ballot anytime up to two days before the election.

In the United States the one-round election in which a plurality is enough for victory normally creates a powerful incentive to limit the number of major candidates. The Russian rules, by contrast, create an incentive for a multiplicity of candidates in the first stages of the election. At a minimum, candidates will receive some funding and free television time. A candidate may also negotiate with another candidate about his price for withdrawing in the last days of the campaign.

There is another factor in 1996. By the beginning of the year it was clear that the Communist candidate, Gennady Zyuganov, would be one of the two candidates in the runoff. It also seemed likely that the second-place winner would receive a relatively small percentage of the votes. A number of candidates could therefore hope they would catch fire and win a place in the runoff. The challenger to Zyuganov, whoever he may be, will raise the specter of a return to the old Communist dictatorship and an aggressive foreign policy. The second round will almost surely turn on whether those in the center of the political spectrum believe they can trust Zyuganov. Thus with the exception of Zhirinovsky, anyone who gets into the runoff has a reasonable chance at victory, and a number of candidates could think they may manage to do so.

In fact, six major candidates collected enough signatures to be certified by the Central Electoral Commission—Svyatoslav Fedorov, Aleksandr Lebed, Grigory Yavlinsky, Boris Yeltsin, Vladimir Zhirinovsky, and Gennady Zyuganov. Another five minor candidates also managed to get on the ballot, and three rejected candidates appealed to courts for inclusion.

Nevertheless, the importance of the presidency and of getting into the second round still creates powerful incentives for alliances to form. The Duma elections have already been important tests of popularity—primaries, if you will—and those who have failed are seeking others with whom to join. Leading candidates of the past—Yegor Gaidar, Boris Fedorov, Nikolai Ryzhkov, Aleksandr Rutskoi, and Viktor Anpilov—have already decided not to run. It is always possible that further alliances will be formed as the election approaches and candidates drop out. Opinion leaders may try to organize strategic voting to try to ensure the strongest anti-Zyuganov opponent.

Boris Yeltsin

Boris Yeltsin has dominated Russian politics since 1989, and he will dominate the 1996 election. It is he who is trying to shape the political landscape through control of television, but the fact that he is trying to define the choice as one of himself against the Communists only strengthens the likelihood that the election will have this character. Zyuganov was a minor politician only a few years ago, and to the extent that he is the front-runner today, it is because Yeltsin has helped him define himself as the main alternative to Yeltsin and Yeltsin has been enormously unpopular.

Yeltsin has not only dominated Russia through this revolutionary period, but had been a significant political figure for the previous decade or more. He, not Zyuganov, was the quintessential party apparatchik of the Brezhnev era. The typical party official did not come through the Young Communist League as did Zyuganov, Mikhail Gorbachev, and Eduard Shevardnadze, but entered party work in early middle age with managerial experience in industry, construction, or agriculture and with a degree in engineering (or less often, agronomy). Yeltsin was a construction engineer who in 1968 became head of the construction department of the regional party committee in Sverdlovsk, one of the most important centers of defense and heavy industries in the country. From 1976 to 1985 he served as the committee's first secretary. He was named party first secretary in Moscow from 1985 to 1987. It was in this post that his relations with Gorbachev became increasingly tense, and in October 1987 he resigned and broke with Gorbachev decisively. His subsequent steps were described in chapter 1.

Yeltsin was elected president of Russia in June 1991, when the country was still a part of the Soviet Union. In the first years of the new Russia, he steadfastly (and unwisely) resisted all pressure to relegitimate himself with a new election. Although economic conditions were poor from his first days in office, he had no credible opposition, and as late as December 1993 he could have won an election and solidified himself in office until the late 1990s. He must have believed the repeated projections of his economic advisers that an economic turnaround was just over the horizon.

At 65 years of age Yeltsin is not a particularly old presidential candidate by world standards. Yet given Russian conditions, he is very old in fundamental ways. His heart problems are well publicized and removed him from public view from late October 1995 until the end of December. His drinking problem has become either worse or better publicized, and some of his best-known drinking lapses are inexcusable for a head of state. For example, he left the prime minister of Ireland standing beside the Russian presidential plane because he was incapable of coming out onto the tarmack, and he left an official visit to China a day early.[3] His health and drinking give him the physical appearance of a man older than his age—he looks far older and weaker than Senator Robert Dole, even though Dole is seven years his senior.

More important, Yeltsin is politically old. All the other credible candidates are members of a postrevolutionary political generation. Zyuganov is the oldest member of the group at 52, except for Svyatoslav Fedorov, but others are members of the Russian baby boom generation. Yavlinsky is 43 years old, Lebed 45, Zhirinovsky 50. Most of the other prominent politicians who are not running—Aleksandr Rutskoi at 49, Boris Fedorov at 38, Yegor Gaidar at 40, Victor Anpilov at 50—are also in this generation.

None of candidates other than Yeltsin and Yavlinsky had positions of any importance at the end of 1990, and even Yavlinsky, as author of the 500-day plan, had visibility rather than power. Those who played major parts in the events of the revolution—Gorbachev, Gaidar, Khasbulatov, Rutskoi—have all fallen into pronounced disfavor. Yeltsin has been by far the most important political presence since 1990, and the public is profoundly tired of him and the turmoil associated with him. They are attracted to new candidates who seem ready to lead Russia into a new era. If Zyuganov is seen as such a baby-boomer, he will win easily; if he and his party are perceived as part of the past, the voters will face a terrible dilemma in their choice.

If Yeltsin's economic program had succeeded, the public would have been delighted to reelect him and allow him to serve in a more ceremonial position. Knowledgeable Russians have been speaking of a political system characterized by the kind of court politics found in the last years of Nikolai II with the domination of figures such as Rasputin. As Yeltsin's popularity continued to diminish because of his economic policy, his relations with his democratic supporters soured and he came to rely increasingly on shadowy figures in his personal entourage, notably Aleksandr Korzhakov, the chief of his security guard.[4] His decision to use troops to try to end the secession of the republic of Chechnia provided the occasion for more open opposition from them, including Gaidar himself.

Despite Yeltsin's political longevity, he is the candidate most difficult to discuss. One cannot describe his party, for he has resisted all advice to form a presidential party. His campaign is totally without organization, other than to the extent he can rely on the local executive in many areas. He has wanted to project an image like that of Charles de Gaulle—a figure who stands above parties and embodies the spirit of the nation.

Yeltsin's platform is also very difficult to describe. Obviously his record is his platform, and in large part people will either be voting on it or on their fears about the Communists. Yet Yeltsin has had a habit of modifying his position in a populist direction on the eve of an election and then abandoning his modifications immediately afterward. He is repeating the first part of that practice in 1996. After the 1995 election, Yeltsin acted as if he were moving decisively to the center and coopting much of the Communist program. He removed the last important young intellectuals favoring rapid economic reform from his government: his old chief of staff, Sergei Filatov; his foreign minister, Andrei Kozyrev; first deputy premier, Anatoly Chubais; and Sergei Shakhrai, his deputy premier for nationality questions were radical academics at the beginning of the 1990s. He also dismissed the chairman of the State Committee of Property.

Yeltsin's new chief of staff, Nikolai Yegorov, is a nationalist with strong ties to the Cossacks. His new foreign minister, Yevgeny Primakov, is a pro-Western foreign specialist but a strong nationalist vis-à-vis "the Near Abroad"—the former republics of the Soviet Union. The new first deputy premier, Kadannikov, was an automobile plant manager who supports an industrial policy and higher tariffs. The new first deputy foreign minister for the Near Abroad, Boris Pastukhov, was first secretary of the USSR Komsomol in the last five years of Brezhnev's life and then chairman of the USSR State Committee of Publishing from 1982 and 1986 before he was exiled as ambassador to Denmark in the first days of perestroika.[5]

Policy seemed to flow in the directions suggested by the appointments. The new finance minister introduced a policy of higher tariffs in the face of IMF objections. Yeltsin pledged to end the deliberate practice of delaying wage payments as a technique of controlling money supply and accused the Ministry of Economy (the new name for Gosplan, the State Planning Committee) of "sabotage" for its policy approving this practice. He stated that "those who do not lament the disintegration of the union do not have a heart" and signed a treaty of union with Belarus and one of economic integration with Kazakhstan, Kyrgyzstan, and Belarus.[6] He was very nationalistic in the face of Chechen terrorism in January.

Major initiatives in privatization were suspended and to some extent reversed.[7] In general, the *Wall Street Journal* has reported, the central government has given "the sort of silence that passes for a bureaucratic go-ahead" to regional administrators who are renationalizing major property. The report described the process in Voronezh at length, suggesting it was peculiar because Voronezh is conservative.[8] In fact, the city of 900,000 people has been a reform stronghold, having elected two extreme radicals, one radical, one moderate radical, and two conservatives to the Russian Congress in 1990. The provincial governor has been a staunch Yeltsin supporter.

In Kemerovo oblast the reformist governor has supported the old management of one of the country's largest iron and steel plants, the Kuznetsk Works in Novokuznetsk, which is using force to prevent new owners from taking control.

The *Financial Times* correspondent attributes the governor's action to corruption and the Communist victory in Kemerovo to popular disgust with him.[9] But cause and effect probably flow in the other direction.

In the district embracing Novokuznetsk, 38 percent of the votes in the December 1995 election were cast for the Communists, 14 percent for Zhirinovsky's Liberal Democrats, and 6 percent for other strong opposition parties. The only semimoderate party with significant support was Svyatoslav Fedorov's Party of Workers' Self-Administration with 14 percent of the vote. Five percent of the voters supported Our Home Is Russia and 4.4 percent each Yabloko and Gaidar's Russia's Democratic Choice. This was the city that elected three extreme radicals to the Russian Congress in 1990 and that was the center of the great coal strikes by miners who were Yeltsin's strongest supporters. It is almost certainly the governor's concern with the city's political reaction to a change in management at the steel plant that was a vital factor in his decision.

Yeltsin's long-time supporters in America are saying that this time he is sincere and that Russian voters can get a Communist-like policy without the Communists,[10] but reporters on the campaign trail are noting considerable skepticism from those with longer memories. There is reason for such skepticism. In March, Yeltsin largely reversed his movement to the center. With great fanfare, he signed a decree—an unconstitutional one at that—allowing agricultural land to be freely sold.[11] This had consistently been the aspect of radical economic reform that was most unpopular. Moreover, when the International Monetary Fund for inexplicable reasons demanded the intensification of his commitment to economic reform just a few months before the election (as it had in September 1993) as the price for its support to get a three-year $10 billion pledge of support.[12] Yeltsin felt obliged to comply. He retreated on the announced tariff increases, and he promised the IMF he would replace oil and natural gas export taxes with taxes on domestic oil, thus raising natural gas and oil prices to world levels by April and July 1996, respectively.[13] Worst of all, the head of the IMF, Michel Camedessus, went on Russian television saying Yeltsin's policy was the only correct one and that Yeltsin would win.[14]

When Yeltsin made his first campaign trip in early April, it replicated his campaign in the referendum of April 1993. For those who listened carefully, he promised the same economic reforms that have been carried out for five years, but greater benefits for every conceivable group and region—more generous scholarships for students, payment of back wages for everyone, an increase in the minimum wage, and larger pensions. But now for the first time he began threatening prison for former premier Nikolai Ryzhkov (a thoroughly decent man) and for university presidents that permitted communists on campus.

Basically, however, Yeltsin's strategy is clear. Just as the Communists have been defining themselves as the one credible anti-Yeltsin alternative, so he has been defining himself as the one credible anti-Communist candidate. One television commercial for Our Home Is Russia in the 1995 Duma election, aired frequently in the week before the election, relied on man-on-the-street interviews, asking whom passersby intended to vote for. Everyone responded with either the Communists or Our Home Is Russia, and the tightness of the race was emphasized to encourage turnout. The spot also showed attractive people of all ages supporting Our Home Is Russia, while Communist supporters were presented as less appealing (an elderly unshaven man, for example).

The 1996 Yeltsin campaign will have a similar character. If it frightens enough voters, Yeltsin may win. But the strategy has drawbacks. Although the Communists have no money for a television campaign, the Yeltsin strategy ensures that they do not need one and that voters will know whom to vote for if they do not want Yeltsin to continue in office. Our Home Is Russia received 10 percent of the vote in 1995. Yeltsin obviously would do better in a runoff, but it remains a very open question whether he can reach the 50 percent threshold.

Gennady Zyuganov and the Communists

On one question, all observers are in agreement. Gennady Zyuganov has achieved a remarkable feat in reorganizing (organizing, really) the Communist Party of the Russian Federation since 1991. Observers debate whether he will be able to win the confidence of enough voters on the second round to obtain a majority, and much of chapter 6 will be devoted to an analysis of that subject. Nevertheless, the mere fact of the debate testifies to the universal agreement that Zyuganov will almost surely be the leading candidate on the first round and will be in the runoff.

Americans take for granted that Zyuganov's Communist party is the successor to the Communist party of the Soviet Union headed by Leonid Brezhnev and Mikhail Gorbachev. In a broad sense this is true, but organizationally the Communist Party of the Russian Federation is the successor to the Russian Republican Communist party. Since the time of Lenin, almost all the republics had a Communist party organization, but the Russian republic was so large that Soviet leaders feared a Russian leader might challenge their power and refused to permit one. When Gorbachev decided in 1990 to decentralize power to the republican level, he was compelled to create a Russian Communist party. But the first leader of the Russian party, Ivan Polozkov, had been more conservative than Gorbachev, and from the beginning Gorbachev had considered the Russian party a challenge to perestroika.

Zyuganov was a member of the Politburo and Secretariat of this new Russian Communist Party—its first Central Committee secretary for ideology (education, culture, science, and propaganda). Two other members of the 1990 Russian Communist leadership were high on the party's list in 1995: Valentin Chikin, then and now editor of the newspaper *Sovetskaia Rossiia*, and Valentin Kuptsov, briefly party leader in 1991 when it was outlawed and now organizational secretary of the party. Both Generals Rutskoi and Lebed, although not now members of the party, were elected members of the first Central Committee of the Russian Communist party in 1990.

Zyuganov followed a career path typical for a Communist party official who would never reach the top ranks. He was born in 1944 in a small village in Orel oblast in south-central Russia near the Ukrainian border. He worked as a rural teacher at the age of 17, but joined the Communist party at age 22 and quickly moved into Young Communist League (Komsomol) work in Orel. He was first secretary of a Komsomol district committee, then a city committee, and finally the Orel Komsomol regional committee (obkom). He moved into the Orel party apparatus, working his way up as secretary and then second secretary of the Orel city party committee. From 1974 to 1983 he was head of the agitation and propaganda department of the Orel party obkom.[15] He then moved to Moscow, serving as an instructor and then head of a sector in the Propaganda Department of the CPSU Central Committee from 1983 to 1989. In 1989 he became a deputy head of a new and broader ideology department and from this post was elected the ideological secretary of the Russian party.[16]

In 1990 Zyuganov was forty-six years old and had made reasonable progress in his career. (At the same age, however, Gorbachev and Yeltsin had been first secretaries of important regional committees—far more important posts.) Before 1990 Zyuganov was far from the circles making important decisions, and even his 1990 post was very much a middle-level one. He was not even a deputy of the USSR or Russian Congress of People's Deputies. Zyuganov was noticeably absent from the dramatic events of August 1991. He did not appear with Yeltsin in front of the White House or with the coup leaders on the Committee for the State of Emergency. Like Gorbachev, he was on vacation, and he was probably acting with deliberate caution. Yet he was not really at a level to be significantly involved. Zyuganov became first secretary of the Russian party only after it was relegalized in 1992.

The Communist party has come a long way organizationally. In 1993 it had no funds, and Zyuganov was afraid of the media. By 1995 its Moscow headquarters had independent offices. Its campaign materials had improved tremendously, the typewritten slips of paper now supplemented with more professional looking posters and pamphlets. The party still avoided television advertising, but it was able to rely more heavily on its own newspapers. Zyuganov was far more comfortable in talking with the media and fielding questions in a press conference. As the only party with a substantial organization and membership, the Communists were able to run a grassroots campaign with ample volunteer labor to distribute materials, identify supporters, and get out the vote. All of this activity will be a feature of the 1996 presidential election.

Zyuganov can deliver an emotional, angry speech to meetings of the party faithful.[17] At the same time he tries to be very reassuring to foreigners. His 1995 statement to Stephen Cohen is typical. All that the Communists want, he said, is "honest, democratic elections, which will result in a moderate, responsible, professional government able to rid the country of the consequences of these neo-liberal policies and introduce policies natural to Russia and its traditions.... Our main goal is to restore law, human rights and the power of the people. All this will be done strictly accoding to the law. We are against repression and expropriation."[18]

Zyuganov also tries to be reassuring in his messages to broader audiences in Russia.[19] Both in the 1993 and 1995 elections, the Communist party had prepared a video to be shown during a portion of its allocated free airtime. The difference in the two videos was a striking indication of the change in image the party was trying to present. In 1993 it focused on the contrast between past Soviet greatness and the current Russian degradation. In 1995 the video portrayed civil war in Russia (Chechenia and Yeltsin's blasting of the parliament building), followed by Zyuganov's picture and the promise, "We are for peace! We are against civil war!" He harkens back to World War II as a time of Red and White reconciliation that he wants to reintroduce.

Some of the Communist platform since 1992 has been predictable. The party has sharply criticized the government's policy of "shock without the therapy" and the deterioration of the social welfare safety net and standards of living. It has emphasized the need to restore the education and health systems and has put representatives of these sectors on its party list to drive home the point.

Unlike Anpilov's party, Zyuganov's Communist party is not wholly opposed to privatization. It emphasizes the importance of creating an economy with many different forms of ownership, including state, cooperative, and private. It points to the Swedish, Austrian, and other mixed economies of Western Europe to illustrate its vision. State ownership would be concentrated in infrastructure industries (energy, transportation, communication) and industries with strategic importance (defense), although the top economic administrator in the leadership also emphasizes the nationalization of the exporting metallurgy industry.[20] Zyuganov also promises a state monopoly of alcohol to increase budget revenues.[21] In other respects, Zyuganov primarily raises issues of equity and corruption in the privatization process. The party pledges to overturn privatization that has taken place illegally but talks about price controls rather than government ownership of small enterprises.

Agriculture is generally ignored in the platforms of other parties, but it has become a focus of attention for the Communists. Although in 1993 they tried unsuccessfully to form a coalition with the Agrarian party, informally they have often cooperated with it. In 1995 the Communists were more independent and aggressive in seeking out the rural voter. They focused on the "scissors"—the gap between the high prices charged agriculture for its inputs and the below-market prices paid by the state for its products. They pledged to end the unfairness by lowering the cost of inputs and protecting farm products from foreign competition. Zyuganov is flatly against the sale of agricultural land but favors a lifetime lease.[22]

In the political sphere the party speaks out for democracy, as of course it always did. Zyuganov attacks the constitution adopted in 1993 for concentrating excessive power in the executive. In the past he enunciated Lenin's slogan "all power to the soviets" to call for a subordination of the executive to the legislature as in Great Britain. In February 1996, however, he abandoned this position. Now he talks about the Russian president having twice the power of the French and four times that of the American and calls for a strengthening of legislative control—specifically the right to confirm cabinet officers.[23] He also is for the establishment of the post of vice-president.[24] Several years ago, Yeltsin appointed all the governors, and now half are elected and half appointed, but Zyuganov promises to have all elected.[25] He does not suggest the constitution be thrown out by revolution or that a new constitutional convention be called. Rather he wants it amended according to the rules. Because the amendment process is difficult, it seems unlikely that he could in any case go much beyond the kind of changes he is now discussing that both the legislature and the regions would likely favor.

The character of the press under a Zyuganov presidency is a crucial unknown. Newspapers have become relatively unimportant because of the inability of the population to afford them. They also depend on government subsidies to buy newsprint. Television has become the all-important media of communication, but the central television is state-controlled while the so-called independent television is scarcely independent. The head of independent television, Igor Malashchenko, is also a member of the ten-person top advisory council of the Yeltsin campaign.[26]

The problem goes beyond the controls imposed by the Yeltsin regime. The Russian journalistic community has had little sense of the need for balance. Newspapers have been linked with political parties—*Pravda* with the Left, for instance, and *Izvestiia* with the extreme Right. The great majority of Russian journalists have been right-wing partisans of radical reform. They have made a monumental mistake in not establishing the precedent of fairness in a democratic media.

If Zyuganov comes to power, he has every legal and moral right to conduct a wholesale change of personnel in the organs dealing with the media and in the state television network. But would he establish a media that for the first time is more or less balanced in its coverage of news and that presents commentary from all shades of political thought? Or would he will follow the Yeltsin government's policy of controlled information, but with a radically different content?

Zyuganov's rhetoric about foreign policy is very nationalist and anti-Western. He talks about the importance of restoring the country's status as one of the world's great powers able to influence international events. In many respects, however, the foreign policy of the Communists is more defensive than expansionist. It condemns the expansion of NATO but does not call for a return to the Warsaw Pact. In January Zyuganov spoke to the European Parliamentary Assembly and called for Russian admission to the Council of Europe. The new Europe, he said, is impossible without Russia.[27]

Zyuganov's insistence that Russia is part of Europe is typical of an apparently important part of his posture. Ideological formulation was always a crucial if esoteric method of communication in the Soviet Union. Whole foreign policy postures in the Stalin period were summarized in seemingly abstruse debates over whether Western governments were partly subordinated to the monopolies, completely subordinated to them, or merged with them.[28] For well over a year after he assumed power, Gorbachev was extremely negative in his characterization of U.S. foreign policy and intentions, but was using subtle, non-Marxist language to signal a major shift in policy.

Zyuganov is similar to the early Gorbachev in his ideological signals. His major book is titled *Derzhava* (Great Power)—very much a non-Marxist term—and he makes the point explicitly in his analysis. Russian foreign policy should not have ideological underpinnings; it should pursue the practical national interests of Russia. These interests, he argues, were the same for prerevolutionary Russia, the Soviet Union, and for Russia on the eve of the twenty-first century.[29] When he does talk about morality in foreign policy, he uses Gorbachev's language, speaking of general human morals (*obshchechelovechskie morali*) rather than class morality, and norms of international legality (*normy mezhdunarodnoi zakonnosti*) rather than class legality. As one Russian observer said, the book "seems to have been written not by the leader of the Communists, but of a clerical movement."[30] Zyuganov also implicitly softens his anti-Western position by pointing to the strategic potential of countries such as India and China as a key reason that Russia be strong.[31] This is the way to imply a need for an alliance with the West.

The Communist foreign economic policy is protectionist, but not autarkic. The party calls for protective tariffs to preserve Russian industry and agriculture, but it does not call for an end to imports. In February, Sergei Glazev, who had been associated with Lebed, worked with the Communists in writing their economic program, and it came to reflect his emphasis on an export strategy.[32] The program advocates an end to reliance on Western economic advisers and international economic organizations such as the IMF, but not to foreign investment.

Although U.S. commentators have been skeptical about the assurances Zyuganov gives foreign investors, he has taken much the same position at home. His harsh criticism of the IMF coupled with a much softer position on foreign investment mirrors attitudes within the electorate as a whole. Even 34 percent of those who were convinced that the West is out to ruin Russia thought foreign investment was a good idea.

Zyuganov, in fact, gives few indications that his foreign policy would be strongly anti-Western. The serious "foreign policy" questions about Zyuganov concern his policy toward the former republics of the Soviet Union. After the 1993 election he began giving much more emphasis to "patriotic" themes. However, he primarily talks about restoring the economic union that linked the former republics of the Soviet Union, and refers to the European Community as an example of the current global trend toward increased integration. He claims that new relations must be based on an entirely new set of principles and agreements which stress equality. The problem is that the union republics were supposedly sovereign in the old Soviet Union, all with ministries of foreign affairs and Ukraine and Belorussia with membership in the United Nations. Whatever Zyuganov's real intentions, it is very difficult to find language that promises the republics more than they already had in theory, but not in practice, in the old Soviet Union, and that can be reassuring to them.

Vladimir Zhirinovsky and the Liberal Democrats

The other well-known opposition figure is Vladimir Zhirinovsky. Zhirinovsky was born in Alma-Ata, Kazakhstan, in 1946 to a Russian mother. His father, who is rumored to have been a Jew, lived in the Western Ukrainian part of Poland from 1920 to 1939, serving in the Polish army. In 1941, after the incorporation of this territory into the Soviet Union, Zhirinovsky's father moved or was sent to Kazakhstan.[33] His son, by his own account, had an unhappy childhood in Kazakhstan, where he felt discriminated against because he was Russian.

Zhirinovsky was educated at the Institute of Asian and African Countries in the Turkish language division. He worked as a military officer in the Transcaucacus, presumably in the intelligence service. He then worked as a translator for the State Committee for Foreign Economic Relations, earned a law degree from Moscow State, and worked for the Mir publishing house. Before his election to the Duma in 1993, he had never held a governing post.

Zhirinovsky, together with Vladimir Bogachev, founded the Liberal Democratic Party of Russia in the summer of 1989 as the first opposition political party in the Soviet Union. The first full congress of the party was held in March 1990 and elected Zhirinovsky party chairman. From the beginning he has been the subject of controversy. He came in a surprise third in the June 1991 election for Russian president, and during the August 1991 coup, he appeared on the balcony of the Moskva Hotel to proclaim his support for the coup. Moscow Mayor Popov demanded that the Liberal Democrats be banned from the December 1993 election for complicity because of Zhirinovsky's inflammatory statements, but this was not done.

During the 1993 parliamentary campaign, Zhirinovsky's party was again the subject of controversy, partly because of Zhirinovsky's flamboyant style and partly because of rumors about his connections to unsavory individuals and groups, including the KGB, Sadam Hussein, and even Yeltsin's administration. Even after his election, Zhirinovsky continued to play to his personal style, throwing orange juice on opponents on national TV and engaging in brawls on the floor of parliament. He was prone to outrageous statements such as that he would help the problem of low birthrates in Russia by fathering a child in each region of the country.

Regardless of style, Zhirinovsky also conveyed a message that a significant segment of the electorate wanted to hear, one of intense nationalism and support for the market coupled with economic populism. Although observers like to emphasize the inappropriateness of the word *Liberal* in the party's name, it has a real economic meaning. The Liberal Democrats are vague about their economic program, but they sharply differentiate themselves from the Communists and Yeltsin on the issue of economic reform. They denounce the Communists more strongly than they do Yeltsin, and they criticize Yeltsin's government more for its implementation of policy than for the policy itself. Although most opposition parties (even Yabloko) voted against the Yeltsin budget in parliament, the Liberal Democrats support it. In 1996 Zhirinovsky seemed to move even closer to Yeltsin both in his words and in the voting of his party in the Duma. Zyuganov began denouncing him, not without some justification, as part of the "party of power" in Moscow.[34]

The Liberal Democratic program devotes far more attention to foreign policy issues than do the Communists, especially foreign policy with the Near Abroad and Eastern Europe, and their solutions are far more drastic. Zhirinovsky may emphasize the cause of ethnic Russians, but it is neither to glorify Russia in its present boundaries nor to recreate an economic union with other former Soviet republics as the Communists advocate. Zhirinovsky long insisted on reestablishing the Russian empire, with boundaries of provinces not following ethnic lines and with all of them equally subordinated to Moscow without a pretense of federalism. Yet in his movement toward Yeltsin in 1996, he began talking about *Rossiia* in Yeltsin's sense, with independence for former Soviet republics but with plebiscites about secession in parts of them populated by Russians.[35]

Finally, the Liberal Democrats show their differences with the Communists on the matter of state institutions. Although the Communist party has been critical of the strong presidency, the Liberal Democrats have consistently supported one. In 1993, although Zhirinovsky criticized the draft constitution for giving too much power to non-Russian regions of the country, he urged his supporters to vote for the document, claiming that the strong presidency is vital for the country. That was one reason he was well financed. He promises to use this office to reestablish a great Russia.

Aleksandr Lebed

During 1995 Aleksandr Lebed was the one politician in Russia with very high and rising approval ratings. In March 1995 he was the one politician with positive confidence ratings: 45 percent against 25 percent who distrusted him and 30 percent who were uncertain. This was up from a 35 percent confidence rating in October 1994. The 45 percent figure was repeated in October 1995.[36]

Given the unpopularity of Yeltsin and the suspicion about Zyuganov and Zhirinovsky, Lebed seemed almost irresistibly on his way to a place in the runoff in the presidential election and likely to victory. A general in the parachute troops with no civilian political experience, he joined with two highly credible civilians, Yury Skokov and Sergei Glazev, at the top of the Congress of Russian Communities (KRO) party.

Born in 1950, Lebed after great effort was admitted to a college that educated officers for the parachute troops and became a career officer. From 1973 to 1981 he commanded a training platoon and then a training regiment at this college. In 1981 and 1982 he commanded a battalion in Afghanistan. After three years in mid-career education in the Frunze Academy, he was appointed commander of a regiment in the Tula Paratroop division, then deputy commander of a larger unit in the division, and in 1989 commander of the division itself. In that capacity he was sent to Baku, Azerbaidzhan, in 1990 to help quell a pogrom against the Armenian minority. His division was also sent to defend the RSFSR Supreme Soviet building during the August 1991 coup. As a reward he was named deputy commander of the paratroops and in June 1992 commander of the 14th army on the Ukrainian-Moldavian border. He became famous when he defended the Russians and Ukrainians living in that section of the republic from the forces of the Moldova nationalist government of the time.

Lebed, Skokov, and Glazev seemed a very well balanced and credible team. Skokov was a former defense industry manager who had been first deputy premier of the Russian Federation under Yeltsin from 1990 to 1991, had run Yeltsin's presidential campaign in 1991, and had served as secretary of the Security Council from 1992 to early 1994. He had been promised the premiership by the president. Glazev had been a minister of foreign trade in the Russian government. He had resigned in response to the dissolution of the Congress and differed with Gaidar over free trade.

Polls conducted in October and November 1995 indicated that the KRO would place in the top three with the Communists and Our Home Is Russia. Instead, it garnered only 4.3 percent of the vote. The party lacked both organization and the financial resources needed to wage an effective television campaign. It also failed to exploit Lebed's popularity effectively, allowing the uncharismatic Skokov to do most of the talking for the group on television. Moreover, although both Skokov and Glazev had views well to the left of Yegor Gaidar, the KRO was often praised as a moderate alternative by Moscow intellectuals. Many in the provinces may have had the suspicion that the former connection of Skokov and Glazev to Yeltsin meant the party was far closer to

Yeltsin than was being acknowledged. In retrospect, even outside observers wondered whether Skokov really was supporting Lebed or was serving Yeltsin. In January 1996 a congress of the KRO nominated Lebed for president. Glazev was absent from this meeting. Skokov, however, did little to promote Lebed or, reportedly, even to encourage the collection of signatures for him to get on the presidential ballot.[37] Rumors swirled through Moscow that Lebed would not make it to the ballot, and sociologists and journalists close to Yeltsin treated Lebed as a candidate whose level of support would not rise much above the level the party received in the December 1995 election.

It was never clear how much of this was objective analysis and how much wishful thinking. Lebed was, however, generally kept off central television to help ensure that the analysis would be backed by reality. Nevertheless, after a good deal of press speculation about an alliance between Lebed, Yavlinsky, and Sviatoslav Fedorov as a "Third Force," Lebed suddenly emerged in early April as the nominee of Sergei Glazev's Democratic Party of Russia. He also emerged in stylish civilian clothes.

Lebed's program has always been murky. Indeed, he uses the language of war: his plans are a secret so the enemy will not be able to defeat them. The Congress of Russian Communities was formed in 1993 to draw together the Russian diaspora in the Near Abroad, and Lebed's record in Moldova made him a natural leader for it. In the 1995 campaign, however, it focused even more on the ethnic communities within Russia, which it treated as a community above ethnic divisions.

In the campaign Lebed concentrated on corruption and foreign policy. He emphasized the new prevalence of crime, which he linked with privatization. He articulated a strongly nationalistic and anti-Western foreign policy. He described the NATO presence in Bosnia as that of a drunken vandal and accused the West of providing the $6.2 billion IMF loan in 1995 to fund the war in Chechnia. His memoir is filled with his utter contempt for Gorbachev, Shevard-nadze, and especially Aleksandr Yakovlev for their betrayal of Russia.[38] He seems far more likely than Zyuganov to have an anti-Western foreign policy.

With Glazev the presumed top economist in any Lebed government, Lebed's economic policy seemed fairly well defined. Glazev launched consistent attacks on the government's economic policy from a Keynesian perspective, supporting a deficit and job creation to promote production. He advocated Russian export promotion like that practiced by the newly industrialized countries of Southeast Asia. Therefore despite his attacks on corrupt privatization, Lebed came across as a man who exhibited a classic combination of nationalism and market-oriented reform.

In 1996 Lebed's language became less nationalistic and more pro-market. He talked about amnesty for those who sent money illegally abroad if they would return it and about Russia's need for "a powerful stratum of owners" for "private property and protection of businessmen."[39] While maintaining his alliance with Glazev, he sought another with Yavlinsky, a Chicago-school monetarist, who would fit very uneasily in the same cabinet with Glazev. But a self-confident contempt ripples through all Lebed's interviews: "the quieter you go," he said, "the wider the trap."[40]

The most striking thing about Lebed in 1996 was the way he implicitly and even explicitly attacked democracy. His memoirs are filled with examples of his decisiveness, but he went further in interviews, including one in 1995 with a westerner.

> Neither I nor my children will live to see democracy because of Russia's mentality. . . . We are trying to leap from totalitarianism to democracy. It doesn't work; there must be a transition period. A democratic state has to be built brick by brick, and people's thinking must change. . . . Pinochet's so-called bloody regime lifted Chile from the ruins, forced everybody to work, revived the economy, restored a feeling of ownership among the people and then legally returned power over to a civilian government. And when Chileans looked around, they were living in a flourishing, civilized country. Right? Right![41]

This approach seemed to hurt him badly in 1995. A majority of those in our poll who said they would support a dictatorship thought he would make a good president, but those who opposed a dictatorship were strongly against him.

But in March 1996 he again told Soviet reporters he was "placid" about Pinochet, although he did not intend "to carve 'I Love Pinochet' into my forehead."[42] Then when he was nominated by the Democratic party, he declared to the convention that "we need a small highly qualified Duma appointed by the president," and apparently did so emphatically.[43] Later he said he did this as a test to prove it did not matter what one said but who one was.

Presumably Lebed thinks he can gain the support of those who favored Yeltsin's economic policy by suggesting he would follow a Pinochet-like policy and gain the support of those against Yeltsin's economic policy by promising a law-and-order campaign against corruption. Let each wonder who is the enemy from whom the "military secrets" in his political strategy are being hidden. Lebed instinctively seems far closer to Glazev and the anti-Americanism of China than to the pro-IMF posture of Chile.

Grigory Yavlinsky and Yabloko

Grigory A. Yavlinsky seems at the opposite end of the political spectrum from the first three candidates. Born in 1952, he is the youngest of the serious candidates, and many think he really is running more to position himself for the next presidential election than to win this one.[44] A labor economist with the equivalent of a Ph.D. in economics from the Moscow Plekhanov Economics Institute, Yavlinsky worked in the State Committee for Labor and Social Problems in the Soviet period. By 1989 he had risen to be head of the Administration of Social Development and Population of the State Committee. He was then hired as a staff member of the Economic Reform Commission of Deputy Premier Leonid Abalkin in 1989.

While on the Abalkin Commission, Yavlinsky and several other young economists drafted a wildly utopian plan that purported to introduce both privatization and market prices in 400 days. Inflation would seemingly be avoided simply by control of the money supply. The plan's time frame was expanded to 500 days by Yeltsin's candidate for premier of Russia, and Yavlinsky himself became deputy premier with responsibility for economic reform in June 1990.

Yavlinsky was the purest of monetarists, and unlike most other reformers, he was sufficiently committed to his principles to resign in November 1990 in protest of Yeltsin's populist policy of monetary expansion.[45] Although the 500-day plan involved both the destruction of the Soviet Union and a much more radical economic program than anything Gaidar attempted, Yabloko still implausibly hearkens back to it as a panacea that would have solved all problems had it been adopted.

By the summer of 1991 Yeltsin began to assemble a group of economists to prepare an economic plan for an independent Russia. The group, chosen by Yegor Gaidar, almost all came from closely associated Academy of Sciences institutes. Yavlinsky had not received his degree in the Academy of Sciences nor ever worked in an Academy institute. The academy economists and Yavlinsky did not develop a cooperative relationship, and as of 1996 still have not. After the August 1991 coup d'etat, Yavlinsky went to work as the deputy chairman for economic reform of the USSR State Committee for Economic

Management. He favored preservation of an economic union in the former Soviet Union, and because G-7 officials were eager for such a union, they were told Yavlinsky was Yeltsin's chief economic adviser and representative on the USSR Committee. In fact, Yeltsin and Yavlinsky had an antagonistic relationship and would continue to have one.

Yavlinsky formed a political party in 1993 with a popular St. Petersburg politician, Yury Boldyrev, and Yeltsin's ambassador to the United States, Vladimir Lukin (by 1995 he had broken with Boldyrev but not Lukin). Letters from the names of the three men were merged to form the informal name of the party, Yabloko, the Russian word for apple. In both 1993 and 1995 the top of the Yabloko party list was filled with Moscow and St. Petersburg intellectuals, and its campaign ads in 1995 were designed for a thinking audience. The ads played on its name Yabloko and one featured Isaac Newton, sitting under his apple tree, being inspired by a falling apple to discover the law of gravity. Posters on bus shelters around Moscow used modernist graphics that conveyed the bloc's message indirectly.

Yabloko and Yavlinsky called themselves centrists and were critical of Gaidar and then of Chernomyrdin for being too heavy-handed and dogmatic in the development and implementation of radical reform. Yet they never created a program that was distinct from Gaidar except in minor detail. In 1995 Yavlinsky refused to join the populist attack on the corruption bred by privatization, but he did pledge to protect established property rights. His criticism of the government's economic programs remained wholly monetarist, this time arguing that money supply could be loosened to increase production.[46] If anything, Yavlinsky seemed to the right of a government that was becoming more populist in 1996.

Although Yabloko portrayed itself in 1995 as the liberal alternative to Yeltsin, it had failed to use the two years since December 1993 to build its electoral organization. It ran candidates in only sixty-nine single-member districts, the fewest of any major party. Fourteen of these were to win—better than the record of Our Home Is Russia or the Liberal Democrats and double its own total in 1993—but all the victories were in the largest cities. If the party ever acquires political skills, it may well survive as a credible successor to Gaidar in opposition to a Communist government, but this will take time.

The Other candidates

Of the other candidates, only one—Svyatoslav Fedorov—seems potentially significant. At age 69 Fedorov is the oldest of the candidates. He was the most famous eye surgeon in the Soviet Union, developing a technique in the 1960s to correct nearsightedness that attracted foreign customers, especially from the Middle East. In 1980 he became the director of the Moscow Research Institute on Eye Microsurgery, and in 1986 he turned it into a "scientific-production association." In recent years he has established a network of franchised eye clinics, and in 1992 he established the Union of Leasees and Entrepreneurs.

In 1995 Fedorov established the Party of Workers' Self-Administration. Fedorov himself is a very pleasant and popular man, and he is openly trying to create an outsider image like Ross Perot's. Indeed, he even visited Perot in Texas to obtain advice. In the 1995 election the Party of Workers' Self-Administration fell just short of the 5 percent minimum required for representation, but Fedorov himself won a seat in a single-member district. His general program and language sound very leftist, and he joined Nikolai Ryzhkov's semi-Communist faction in the Duma. Yet Fedorov's implicit model of workers' self-administration seems to stem from his own franchises rather than any traditional socialism.

One could imagine Fedorov doing very well as a stop-Zyuganov candidate. His language is the most leftist of any of the centrist or right-wing candidates, and he could appeal to many, especially women, who have been anti-Yeltsin but leery of the Communists. Yet his record suggests he would be pro-market. His problems are twofold: first, of course, he has had no administrative experience and, like Perot, offers little in the way of a concrete program; second, Yeltsin's control of television is likely to give him little chance of reaching a mass audience with the kind of television appeals that Perot or Stephen Forbes made.

None of the other five candidates is at all serious. For obscure reasons, Mikhail Gorbachev has decided to run and is unlikely to gain more than 1 percent of the vote. Aman Tuleev, a populist leader from West Siberia, is running as a second Communist candidate in case anything happens to Zyuganov. Yury Vlasov is a former weight lifting champion who espouses a nationalist position, while Vladimir Bryntsalov, a millionaire, and Martin Shakkum, an associate of radical economist Stanislav Shatalin, are on the right wing. Three other insignificant candidates—Galina Starovoitova, Lev Ubozhko, and Viacheslav Ushakov—were denied a place on the ballot because of alleged irregularities on their signature lists—but they are appealing to the courts. One or more may be registered.

6

The Presidential Election:
The Strength of the Candidates

After the December 1995 election, the Duma remained as weak an institution as beforehand. In addition, in itself, the 1995 election had a relatively small impact on policy. The opposition parties continued to avoid confrontation with the government as all eyes focused on the presidential election scheduled for June 16, 1996. The parties' inaction was facilitated by Yeltsin's removal of several of the most radical members of the government and by apparent changes in policy on privatization, foreign economic policy, Chechnia, and the former republics of the Soviet Union.

In December 1995 the public had not yet concentrated on the presidential election. Our study asked about that election in a definitive way—"For whom do you think you will vote?"—and found that only 20 percent of respondents had an answer. The top choice received the support of only 3.3 percent of the respondents. Most Moscow polling agencies worded the question in a way that tried to push respondents to a choice, and the surveys generally found that the top choice received about 10 percent of the vote. One such poll at the end of January 1996 found 11 percent for Zyuganov, 8 percent for Yavlinsky, 7 percent for Zhirinovsky, 6 percent for Lebed, 5 percent for Yeltsin, 4 percent for Chernomyrdin, and 4 percent for Svyatoslav Fedorov.[1]

By the beginning of April the Western press was reporting that Yeltsin was enjoying a surge of popularity. They were citing the results of surveys conducted by several Russian polling agencies in late March. The results most often cited were those by the All-Russian Center for Public Opinion Research presented in table 6-1.

Yet Lee Hockstader, the experienced *Washington Post* correspondent who reported these results in an article covering Yeltsin's first campaign trip, decided

Table 6-1. Distribution of Support for Russian Presidential Candidates According to All-Russian Center for Public Opinion Research, 1996

Percent

Candidate	January	February	Mid-March	End of March	Mid-April
First round					
Zyuganov	20	24	25	25	26
Yeltsin	8	11	15	18	18
Yavlinsky	13	9	11	9	10
Zhirinovsky	10	12	9	9	8
Lebed	10	8	8	10	10
S. Fedorov	8	7	7	7	8
Chernomyrdin	7	5	4	3	4
Gaidar	3	4	3	3	3
Gorbachev	1	1	1	1	1
Another	3	2	1	1	1
Against all	2	3	4	4	2
Difficult to answer	14	13	10	9	10
Second round: Yeltsin and Zyuganov					
For Yeltsin	19	21	24	29	28
For Zyuganov	33	34	32	30	29
Against both	20	22	21	17	18
Will not vote	15	15	12	12	15
Difficult to answer	13	10	10	12	10

Source: Yury Levada (director of the All-Russian Center for Public Opinion Research), "Do vyborov vosem' nedel'. Razryv mezhdu Zyuganovym i Yel'tsinym sokhraniaetsia," *Izvestiia,* April 16, 1996, p. 2.

to end his article with a statement by a young man working as a driver: "When Yeltsin is talking to people, everyone is smiling and nodding as if they like him. In reality, everyone is going to vote against him."[2] There is reason for caution.

The All-Russian Center for Public Opinion Research historically has become politicized and has erred in overestimating the support for radical candidates. In this case the pattern of results itself is worrisome. A person with experience with Russian sociological surveys—and even the nonexpert who has read this book carefully—knows that Russian respondents have a strong tendency to answer "difficult to answer" when they are undecided. A consistent 9 to 10 percent "undecided" answer in March and April is simply not credible for the first-round preferences when the names of the candidates were not even known.

Part of the answer is found in an earlier article on the mid-March study: the figures apply only to the 65 percent of the respondents who say they will vote, and only 40 percent of those offering a choice said they felt sure they would vote for the candidate they named.[3] In short, the interviewers were not pushing for their preference those who were uncertain about their intention to vote, because the actual turnout is very likely to be more than 65 percent. But the interviewers clearly were putting great pressure on the 65 percent who said they would vote to name a choice. In such a situation, the undecided person is likely to give a respectable familiar name. Yeltsin should have been the prime beneficiary of such a methodology.

In addition, the continued inclusion of two noncandidates on the list— Chernomyrdin and Gaidar—clearly was designed to lessen the support for moderate or radical anti-Yeltsin candidates such as Yavlinsky and make Yeltsin's lead over the third-place candidate larger than it is. Zhirinovsky is placed too high for his percentage so as to push further down the list the real challengers to Yeltsin for the second spot—Lebed and even Fedorov.

Given all the hostility to Yeltsin and the 35 percent support for leftist parties in December, it is even more unbelievable that Zyuganov's support would only increase from 26 percent on the first round to 29 percent on the second. Even after the exclusion of the third of respondents who say they would not vote on the first round, a third of the first-round voters have purportedly decided not to vote for either candidate on the second round. Only 43 percent of the total electorate (that is, including the 35 percent "nonvoters" of the first round) is going to vote for someone in the second round, and only 37 percent of these voters have a preference. With 70 percent of the population likely to vote and Levada informally working for the president, it is obvious that he probed the attitudes of the huge number of respondents not included in this 37 percent. It is also obvious why he did not publish the results of this part of the study: the missing 63 percent is not pro-Yeltsin.

More believable results were found in a poll conducted at the end of March by the Ramir agency: a 27 percent to 19 percent lead for Zyuganov, with 9 percent for Lebed. Zyuganov was ahead of Yeltsin in a hypothetical runoff by a 40 percent to 30 percent margin.[4] This latter result approximates the margin that would have been predicted on the basis of the December 1995 Duma election. These figures also seem accurate in suggesting that a third of the electorate is still undecided.

By all the evidence, the undecided are very unfavorable in their evaluation of Boris Yeltsin as president, but also suspicious of the Communists. It is by no means self-evident whom the undecided will eventually choose. The best way to assess what is taking place—and to evaluate the results in retrospect after the election is over—is to try to examine the cross-pressures under which the unhappy Russian voters are operating. That will be the purpose of this chapter.

The Balance of Forces in the Spring of 1996

The 1995 election was a party election, and it had far more parties than will be present on the presidential ballot. It also had one fewer. Boris Yeltsin supported no one in the election, but he was out of sight—officially because of his heart problems. Nevertheless, the election was peculiar in that the names of the party leaders were on the ballot together with their party, and most parties actually were extensions of their leaders.

Our questionnaire in both 1993 and 1995 asked respondents if they had heard of a number of parties (the 1993 questionnaire included all of them) and if they had an evaluation. They were asked to say whether they evaluated the party positively, more positively than negatively, more negatively than positively, or negatively. The results for the seven most relevant parties in 1995 are presented in table 6-2. Like the ballot, our survey listed the name of the leader. As a result, we usually received evaluations of leaders as well as parties. We also asked individual questions to evaluate attitudes toward Boris Yeltsin and Aleksandr Lebed as persons.

Table 6-2 is a good place to begin the analysis of the 1996 election, although it must be used with care. Even leaving aside the fact that attitudes can and will shift during a six-month campaign, the results had a very mixed relation to voting choice in 1995. The 22 percent positive rating of the Communist party and the 11 percent positive rating of Zhirinovsky's Liberal Democrats were identical with the vote each received, but other parties received a rating that was higher than their ultimate share of the vote.

Nevertheless, several points are reasonably clear. First, except in their attitudes toward Vladimir Zhirinovsky and Boris Yeltsin, a large proportion of the population was still uncertain about the contenders. Given Yeltsin's highly unfavorable ratings, there is much potential for major shifts in voter preference. Second, Zhirinovsky has no chance of being elected president and almost none of reaching the runoff. The number of his "don't know" responses fell nearly in half from 1993 to 1995, but the absolute number of his positive ratings declined while his negative evaluations soared. Moreover, Zhirinovsky has no visible reservoir of support among particular groups of the population. Table 6-3 shows the waning of his popularity across all occupational groups. The result is the

Table 6-2. Evaluation of Political Parties and of Yeltsin and Lebed as Persons, December 1995

Percent

Party or individual	Don't know	Positive	More positive than negative	More negative than positive	Negative
Women of Russia	35	32	18	6	9
Communist (Zyuganov)	31	22	12	10	26
Yabloko (Yavlinsky)	40	17	16	10	17
Congress of Russian Communities (Lebed)	47	16	13	8	17
Lebed as a person[a]	43	8	16	19	15
Our Home Is Russia (Chernomyrdin)	31	14	15	13	28
Liberal Democrats (Zhirinovsky)	20	11	8	10	51
Russia's Democratic Choice (Gaidar)	30	10	11	13	36
Worker Self-Administration (Fedorov)	52	18	13	6	11
Yeltsin as a person[a]	12	3	13	29	44

a. The question about Lebed asked if respondents thought he would be a good president; that about Yeltsin asked if respondents approved of his activity as president. The answers were correspondingly different, but were in five categories comparable to those on evaluation of parties.

same when respondents are classified by age or the population of the area in which they live.

Third, with the Communists seemingly assured a place in the runoff, the most interesting fact about the first round is that the three parties likely to challenge Yeltsin for the second spot all received a net positive rating (merging "more positive than negative" with "positive"). To be sure, the huge percentage of "don't know" responses shows the softness of the support for any of the three, and despite Yavlinsky's ratings, the Yabloko party dropped from 7.9 percent of the vote in 1993 to 6.9 percent in 1995.[5]

The most interesting figures deal with General Lebed, about whom a special question was included: "Independent of your own preference, do you think that Aleksandr Lebed would be a good president?" Eight percent answered "definitely yes," 16 percent "generally yes," 19 percent "generally no," and 15

Table 6-3. Evaluation of the Liberal Democrats, by Respondent Occupation, 1993, 1995

Percent

Occupation	Don't know		Positive		More positive than negative		More negative than positive		Negative	
	1993	1995	1993	1995	1993	1995	1993	1995	1993	1995
Manager	24	11	15	12	11	8	13	10	37	59
Professional	25	15	11	6	12	6	14	10	38	64
White collar	31	13	15	4	12	8	11	15	31	60
Worker	38	19	19	12	10	9	8	13	25	48
Peasant	40	27	14	16	10	14	6	7	29	37
Retiree	50	26	15	12	7	7	7	8	22	48
Total population	37	20	15	11	10	8	9	10	28	51

percent "definitely no." Twenty-four percent approval would be enough to make the runoff, and the 43 percent of respondents without an opinion provide an enormous reservoir of potential support. This is especially true because of Lebed's high approval ratings in 1995.

General Lebed's problem is that those who approved of the Communists thought he might make a good president by a 35 percent to 29 percent margin and those voters are voting Communist. Only 20 percent of respondents who were negative about the Communists believed he might make a good president; 49 percent who were negative toward the Communists thought he would not. On the surface, Lebed seems to need to persuade people he is committed to democracy if he is to have a chance. That seems not to be his current strategy.

Fourth, the real question about the election is people's attitude toward the Communists. In the 1995 Duma elections the Communists received twice as many votes as any other party and had a positive rating from 34 percent of the population, including the undecided. They also, however, had strong negative ratings. Without a doubt, Gennady Zyuganov has a solid core of supporters; the question is whether he can win enough centrist voters to win a majority in a two-person runoff.

The Strength of the Communists

It is easy enough to summarize the major issues in the 1996 election. Much of the population is suspicious of the Communists. Television coverage of Zyuganov will be highly unfavorable, while the coverage of Yeltsin's other challengers will be minimal in the extreme. If Yeltsin and Zyuganov become the two candidates in the runoff, most of the centrist and nationalist candidates will endorse Yeltsin or perhaps counsel their supporters to vote "none of the above," which is an option on the ballot. The question is whether these factors will overcome the enormous grassroots strength of the Communists and the very strong desire of the people to have a new president.

Many Moscow observers have an instinctive feeling that ultimately voters will choose the known over the unknown. In early 1990 few expected Yeltsin would be elected chairman of the Russian Supreme Soviet. No one in early 1991 would have expected he could have succeeded in breaking up the Soviet Union by the end of the year and take over Gorbachev's job. Few thought he would have won majority approval of his social policies in the April 1993 referendum.

Memories of the 1993 referendum are especially strong. Yeltsin shamelessly used his control of television to present one side of the issue, made innumerable promises to everyone, and defined himself as the only defense against chaos and a restoration of Communism. He is following essentially the same formula this year, and few Moscovites want to bet it will not work again. It certainly will work in Moscow itself.

But there are major differences between April 1993 and June 1996. First, three years have passed. Economic conditions are much worse, and Yeltsin's approval ratings are much lower. In 1993 he successfully portrayed the Congress of People's Deputies as the source of Russia's problems, but in 1996 the new constitution and the tactics of the Duma leaders have made it clear that Yeltsin is fully responsible for what has occurred. He has repeatedly promised, and his promises have seldom been carried out.

Second, in early 1993 even Yeltsin's critics saw him as a vigorous leader, but in 1996 no one thinks he is healthy enough or energetic enough to provide sustained leadership for four years. One Western news correspondent who reported his first campaign in relatively favorable terms has written that "Boris Yeltsin is stirring from his deep political coma." Another has commented, "he has suddenly become very public and highly energetic."[6] The words *suddenly* and *political coma* accurately reflect that he has seemed like Brezhnev did in his later years. Even if he maintains his current energy level for two months and does not have another incident with his health or another visible problem with his drinking, no one thinks that as a leader he would be any more vigorous after the election than he has been the past few years.

The best that can be said is that Yeltsin may serve as a largely ceremonial president and that his premier may be able to achieve a turnaround in the economy now that most of the radicals have been driven out of the government.

A population that lived through a decade of stagnation under the generally nonfunctioning Brezhnev, Chernenko, and Andropov will have to believe that another four years of a leader with severe physical problems will still witness a dramatic improvement in the situation.

More important, the Communist party has changed and so too has the perception of it. In April 1993 the Congress of People's Deputies did not have a Communist majority, and there were virtually no ties between the Communists of Russia faction in the Congress and the Communist party outside the Congress. The party did not have a strong grass roots organization, and it had not succeeded in melding its nationalist and economic appeals. It was far more critical of economic reform than the majority of the population.

Today the party is much better organized, and its message is far better tuned. The public has become more critical of economic reform, while the party has moderated its opposition to it. Thus the Communists are much closer to the mainstream of public opinion. Chechnia has allowed them to emerge as the opponents of military force and civil war.

Those who claim that the Communists have little chance sometimes say they are a party of the countryside and small town. Even if that were true (and the biggest story of the 1995 election was the enormous increase in Communist support in the industrial Urals and West Siberia), it often is forgotten that half the Russian population lives in villages and towns with fewer than 100,000 people. It is said that the Communists are primarily the party of the retirees, but retirement begins at age 55 for women and 60 for men, and 31.5 percent of the electorate is 55 or older. The oldest members of the baby boom generation are only five years away from turning 55, and another 14 percent of the electorate is between 45 and 55.

Many still hold an unfavorable opinion of the Communist party, but we should not forget that victory in the runoff requires only 50.1 percent of the vote. Many voters in the 1996 U.S. presidential election, as in all such elections, are not enthralled by either candidate, but ultimately they will make a choice and someone will win. Large numbers of Russian voters will also feel disenchanted about the choices in the runoff, but someone will win.

If the election is seen in this light, the Communists look to be in a very strong position for the 1996 election if they run a strong campaign and face a weak candidate such as Yeltsin. Let us take the 3,827 respondents in our survey and think of them as a microcosm of the electorate. Assume that voter turnout will be 70 percent of the electorate. That would mean 2,679 voter-respondents, with the victor needing 1,340 to win. At the time of the survey 425, or 22 percent of those with an opinion, reported their intention to vote Communist. If the sample was representative of the electorate, then another 140 decided to vote Communist between the interview and the election, and 320 voted for other leftist parties. That is a total of 885 respondents, and it is hard to imagine that Zyuganov will get less than 800 of them in June.

If those intending to vote Communist are excluded, 483 of the other respondents evaluated the Communists positively and 413 more positively than negatively. If we subtract the 460 who presumably voted for the Communists and other leftist parties, we are left with 435 respondents. If they behaved like the rest of the population, then 290 voted for nonleftist parties—the great majority for a nationalist or centrist party—and 170 did not vote. Given the strength of Zyuganov's get-out-the-vote campaign, he should get at least 200 of these respondents and maybe between 250 and 300. The minimum estimates of 800 former leftist voters and of 200 others favorable to the Communists brings him to 1,000 votes and the maximum estimates to 1,100—from 75 percent to 81 percent of the total he needs.

Obviously if Zyuganov is going to win, he needs to pick up the rest of his hypothetical majority from persons who evaluated his party negatively or more negatively than positively in December 1995 or were undecided.

Some of those who expressed an unfavorable judgment about the Communists approved of Yeltsin or many of the policies he favored (or both). These voters are irrevocably lost to Zyuganov unless Yeltsin does something to discredit himself. There is, however, another group that has disapproved of the Communists but is close to them on policy issues and disapproves of Yeltsin as well. These are the voters who will decide the election.

Table 6-4 makes clear how difficult, even desperate, Yeltsin's position is. One can see how the respondents who disapprove of the Communists could hypothetically swing in mass to Yavlinsky, especially if the Communists did not have much time to build a case against him. General Lebed also has a good basis for building support among these disaffected. However, Yeltsin's negative ratings *even among those who dislike the Communists* are nearly 70 percent, even excluding the undecided.

To return to Zyuganov's task of building a majority, we estimated he might have 1,000 to 1,100 of the 1,340 voters he needs, not considering those with a negative or undecided opinion toward the Communists. Of those who absolutely disapproved of the Communists, 377 also flatly disapproved of Yeltsin, as did

Table 6-4. Attitudes toward other Candidates from Respondents with "Negative" or "Don't Know" Views toward the Communists

Percent

Other parties and leaders	Attitude toward other parties and leaders				
	Positive	More positive than negative	More negative than positive	Negative	Don't know
Negative attitude toward Communists					
Yabloko (Yavlinsky)	25	18	8	29	19
General Lebed as a person	6	13	23	27	31
Boris Yeltsin as a person	4	19	30	38	10
More negative than positive attitude toward Communists					
Yabloko (Yavlinsky)	24	30	27	5	14
General Lebed as a person	6	18	27	17	33
Boris Yeltsin as a person	2	20	40	30	9
"Don't know" attitude toward Communists					
Yabloko (Yavlinsky)	9	7	5	5	74
General Lebed as a person	7	12	13	9	60
Boris Yeltsin as a person	4	10	27	40	19

109 of those with a more negative than positive attitude toward the Communists and 461 of those undecided about them. That is a total of 946 respondents. Another 763 had more negative than positive attitudes toward Yeltsin. Zyuganov would need 300 to 400 of these 1,709 respondents to win. Of these, 138 expressed an intention to vote for an extreme nationalist party in 1995 and 118 for Zhirinovsky. Zyuganov scarcely seems to face an insurmountable task in finding the necessary 300 to 400 persons.

The same point can be made if one looks at policy issues. If only respondents with a negative or more negative than positive opinion of the Communists are considered, 404 totally disapproved of the privatization of large enterprises and 359 of any type of sale of land, even regulated sale. Respondents who were undecided about the Communists included 309 who were totally against the privatization of big factories and 417 who absolutely disapproved of the sale of land. Zyuganov needs less than half the votes of these hardliners on these issues to win.

This is, of course, an analysis based entirely on attitudes in December 1995, and attitudes will change somewhat before June 1996. Yeltsin does, after all, have control of television, and in the past he has had the ability to change his image. But the public's attitude toward the Communists became more favorable from 1993 to 1995 despite Yeltsin's control of the media, and Zyuganov will try to promote a continuation of the trend.

The most alarming—even astonishing—poll results for Yeltsin were published in April from an unscientific survey by the relatively radical newspaper, *Argumenty i fakty*. In February and March the newspaper asked its readers to fill out a questionnaire with their preferences for who should fill various government posts. More than 100,000 responses were received, although, of course, they were completely nonrandom. The results were almost always what was to be expected: Yavlinsky was the choice for premier (with Chernomyrdin in second place and Gaidar in third), Anatoly Chubais for first vice premier, Boris Fedorov for minister of finances, and so forth. Right-wing personalities dominated all the top spots related to economics. However, 21.4 percent favored Zyuganov for president and 20.1 percent Yeltsin, with 11 percent favoring Yavlinsky.[7] If Yeltsin is in this much trouble in his political base, one can imagine his problems with those with other views.

Finally, we should not forget the importance of organization and intensity. When it is said that the Communists are the only organized party in Russia, some people have the image of a tightly built structure of party secretaries. When there are competitive elections, however, the more important factor is the presence of activists who will campaign for the party, try to persuade indifferent friends to participate, and help in get-out-the-vote campaigns. The Leninist conception of a party member always required that members not simply vote for the party or pay dues but actively help it achieve its goals. In the modern world, that means campaign work.

As table 6-5 shows, the supporters of the Communists have been the most intense in their convictions about the importance of the election and the most active in their interest and political participation. This is a matter of great importance. The type of television campaign that Our Home Is Russia ran in 1995 and that Yeltsin is running this year ensures that the Communist party will have no problem with name recognition and none identifying itself as the only credible opposition to Yeltsin. The large network of members and activists means that voters will be meeting real people—often friends and neighbors—who will reassure them that Zyuganov can be trusted and that the media treatment of him is misleading.

Table 6-5. Indicators of Political Interest among Voters, by Party Affiliation, December 1995

Percent

Indicator	Communist	Nationalist	Right-wing	Centrist
Interested in campaign	54	48	45	36
Consider election results very important	65	63	57	53
Discussed politics every day during the last week	29	27	19	19
Watched television election coverage every day during the last week	47	39	32	32
Read newspaper election coverage every day during the last week	15	14	11	7
Listened to radio election coverage every during the last week	31	27	21	19
Was exposed to campaigning at workplace during the last week	30	31	23	20
Attended meetings with candidates during the last week	10	7	5	3

Potential Sources of Communist Growth in Support

There are a number of geographic and demographic groups among which the Communist appeal could gain support. The first, of course, is people living in the geographic areas and population concentrations where the Communists are already strong. More than half the electorate lives in cities of less than 100,000 people. Economic reform has harmed them, and their mood in 1993 was very much opposed to the people in power. The transfer of their allegiance from the Liberal Democrats to the Communists was well under way in 1995. It is precisely in such places where organization, personal political campaigning, and get-out-the-vote techniques—the strength of the Communists—are likely to be especially effective.

Second, support for the Communists may also very well grow among women. The centrist vote is disproportionately female (table 6-6). Although women's income has fallen further behind men's since independence, their voting behavior has been more moderate, as has their evaluation of the Communist party (table 6-7).

Table 6-6. Voting, by Gender and Party Type, 1995

Percent

Gender	Parties			
	Right-wing	Left-wing	National	Centrist
Male	26	37	24	13
Female	26	33	14	28

Note: Our survey results were very close to the actual voting totals for all the major parties, but they were less accurate on some of the minor parties. In particular, our respondents reported twice as much support for Women of Russia than they were to receive. (Interviewers reported that many older women who likely would not vote named Women of Russia—the first entry on the list they were handed—as their party). One-half of the Women of Russia answers are removed from the table.

One major reason for women's political behavior is the "babushka effect." Widows often live with their children, so their economic interests and their views may be influenced by them. Still, it is amazing that 58 percent of men and only 47 percent of women voted for strongly oppositional parties in 1995 when women have been more opposed to economic reform from the beginning and when reform has hurt them so much economically. Women are very suspicious of the nationalist parties and much more attracted to the social welfare position of the centrists. The Communists have to persuade women that the Yeltsin of the Chechen adventure is a more dangerous nationalist than the Communists, who have spoken of peace since Lenin's time. And the party's social welfare position should at a minimum bring the proportion of women favoring the

Table 6-7. Evaluation of Communist Party, by Gender and Age, 1995

Percent

Age	Men		Women	
	Don't know	Positive	Don't know	Positive
18–24	35	16	38	18
25–34	35	22	36	20
35–44	24	35	32	29
45–54	20	37	24	44
55–64	24	52	30	43
65 or older	17	54	40	44

Table 6-8. Evaluation of Communist Party, by Respondent Occupation, 1993, 1995

Percent

Occupation	Don't know		Positive		More positive than negative		More negative than positive		Negative	
	1993	1995	1993	1995	1993	1995	1993	1995	1993	1995
Manager	36	20	11	21	9	15	12	11	33	33
Professional	40	23	10	14	11	12	8	14	31	36
White collar	57	26	8	19	7	16	8	10	20	29
Worker	56	32	10	19	7	12	5	11	23	27
Peasant	62	25	17	37	11	19	1	6	9	14
Retiree	57	34	15	34	7	11	4	6	17	17
Total population	53	31	11	22	8	12	6	10	23	26

Communists closer to the proportion of men in opposition. That alone would give the party victory.

A third potential source of support for Communists are the workers in northern cities whose fundamental interests are in a national industrial policy and protectionism. Table 6-8 shows the evolution in the attitudes toward Communists by occupational groups between 1993 and 1995. The mass of data may make it difficult for the reader to focus on the most relevant figures, but the most useful approach is to add the 1995 "positive" and "more positive than negative" evaluations of the various groups.

Obviously, the Communists have had difficulty picking up support among the professionals, and the fact that westerners have contact only with this group is one reason they have had such a hard time understanding the change in attitudes toward the Communists on the part of society as a whole. However, nothing is more astonishing in any of the tables in this book than that only 31 percent of workers evaluated the Communist party favorably in 1995, compared with 36 percent of managers, 35 percent of white-collar employees, and 26 percent of professionals.

The total of votes obtained by each party in each county, borough, and city in Russia is available, and it shows an amazing variation in the vote in boroughs and towns that are totally dominated by big industrial plants.[8] Clifford Gaddy describes several of these in his book. Lenin borough in Saratov is his archetype of "a defense industry borough": in December 1995 it voted 25 percent for the Communists, 8 percent for other leftist parties, 25 percent for nationalist parties, and 7 percent for reform parties. The voting behavior in Perm, the defense city to which Gaddy has given the most attention, was very different: 10 percent Communist, 5 percent other leftist, 17 percent nationalist, and 37 percent reform. The famous tank city of Nizhnii Tagil was similar to Perm: 8 percent Communist, 7 percent other leftist, 10 percent nationalist, and 25 percent reform.

Cities based on other industries also varied greatly in their voting behavior. The steel city of Cherepovets in the conservative Vologda region voted 11 percent for the Communists and 10 percent for Zhirinovsky, while the steel borough in Novokuznetsk in West Siberia voted 30 percent for the Communists and 16 percent for Zhirinovsky. The coal city of Prokopevsk in West Siberia gave 47 percent of its votes to the Communists and 16 percent to Zhirinovsky, while the coal city of Shakhti in Rostov region in the conservative south gave the two parties 17 percent and 14 percent respectively. The borough of the huge auto works in Toliatti voted 9 percent for the Communists and 17 percent for Zhirinovsky, while that of the huge auto works in nearby Nizhne Novgorod voted 11 percent for the Communists and 10 percent for Zhirinovsky.

Especially given his major gains in support in the Urals and West Siberia in 1995, it is hard to imagine that Zyuganov will not make a major breakthrough with the workers in 1996. It is not plausible that more than a third of workers will still have no opinion of Zyuganov in June 1996 and that many will not turn in his direction as the closest equivalent of a social-democratic party. Of course many of them are women workers.

Ultimately, however, the extent of the shift will be decided by the baby boomers. In Russia far more than America, World War II had a devastating effect on those born in the early 1920s and depressed birthrates. The high death rate of young men during the war made the baby boom more prolonged and its peak later than in the United States, but the generation is still very large. Its first members are now turning 50. In the United States, we are very aware that many baby boomers see Robert Dole as too old and that their attention is increasingly focused on the health system during their retirement years.

The crucial question is how aware the baby boomers are of the near collapse of the Russian health system in the past five years. Average life expectancy of Russian men has fallen from 64.0 in 1989–90 and 63.5 in 1991 to 58.9 in 1993 and 57.3 in 1994.[9] (Life expectancy in 1994 for U.S. white males was 73 years.) The problem is not so much an increase in infant mortality as an increase in the death rates of the middle-aged and elderly. As table 6-9 shows, the age-specific mortality rates for the middle-aged—the older baby boomers—have virtually doubled.

Table 6-9. Mortality Rates in Russia per 1,000 Population, by Age and Gender, 1990–94

Age	1990	1991	1992	1993	1994
Men					
40–44	7.6	8.0	9.8	13.3	15.2
45–49	11.7	11.6	13.8	17.8	20.8
50–54	16.1	16.6	19.4	26.3	29.1
55–59	23.4	23.3	25.3	31.3	38.2
60–64	34.2	34.6	36.9	46.3	61.0
65–69	48.0	47.3	49.4	59.4	64.0
Women					
40–44	2.4	2.6	2.8	3.7	4.2
45–49	3.8	3.8	4.2	6.4	8.2
50–54	5.4	6.6	8.1	7.9	8.0
55–59	8.6	8.6	9.1	10.9	12.3
60–64	13.5	13.6	14.4	16.7	18.4
65–69	22.0	22.0	22.6	26.6	27.1

Source: *Rossiiskii statisticheskii ezhegodnik* (Moscow: Goskomstat, 1996), p. 33.

In 1987 the average male 50-year-old Russian could expect to live an additional 21.3 years and the average male 60-year-old 14.7 years.[10] These were already well below the comparable American figures of 27.1 and 19.1 for white men of those ages. Yet by 1993 the life expectancy of the Russian man of 50 had fallen further to 18.8 years and that of the 60-year-old to 13.2 years.[11] These figures surely decreased further in 1994 and 1995.

The average reader probably has no conception what the figures in table 6-8 mean. If the death rates for those age 40 to 70 in 1990—already high by Western standards—had been maintained in 1994, about 100,000 fewer women and 200,000 fewer men of this age group would have died than actually did. If all age groups are taken into account, 400,000 more men and 200,000 more women died in 1994 alone than would have died if the mortality rates had remained what they had been in 1990—a total of 600,000 people. In addition, some 150,000 "excess" deaths occurred in 1991, 300,000 in 1992, and 450,000 in 1993. The total—1.5 millions extra deaths in four years—is considerably larger than the number Stalin killed in the Great Purge between 1937 and 1939.

The Outcome of the First Round

In the American presidential election of 1980, President Jimmy Carter had a lead in the polls over Ronald Reagan as late as the end of summer. The Democratic candidate, Michael Dukakis, had a large lead over George Bush in July 1988, and President Bush began the 1992 election with a similar lead over Bill Clinton. Obviously presidential voting intentions expressed in public opinion polls are very volatile even in a stable political system dominated by two parties that have existed for more than a century. As the beginning of the chapter noted, according to the leading polling agency in Russia in mid-April—two months before the election—35 percent of the respondents claimed they would not vote, 10 percent of the rest said they were undecided, and 40 percent of the "decided" said they might change their vote. That meant that only 35 percent claimed to have made a firm decision. But they did not know who the candidates would be, they had been exposed to only a small part of the campaign, and the views of some of them were surely subject to change.

Like the Russian people, the authors of this book face enormous problems in judging the outcome, for the book must go to press six weeks before the election is held and just as the registration of candidates is being finished. Worst of all, we cannot be sure about how much of the campaign the public will see.

On his first electioneering trip to Siberia, Gennady Zyuganov told his audience that, among other things, both he and Stalin had great respect for the Russian Orthodox Church. In the campaign as portrayed both on state-controlled and "independent" NTV television, however, Zyuganov never went to Siberia or said anything about the Russian Church. Other candidates, except for Yeltsin, have been rendered even more invisible.[12] With the head of the independent network also serving as an official adviser on the Yeltsin campaign, this disparity between the campaign on the hustings and the campaign the viewer sees is likely to remain strong.

As in 1995, Zyuganov is the only major candidate who seems to have a Westernlike strategic sense of how to run a campaign. During the first months of 1996 he consolidated his position on the Left. He worked to ensure that a number of left-wing candidates did not run but instead endorsed him. The most notable were Nikolai Ryzhkov, the former Soviet premier who had been the Communist party candidate in the 1991 Russian presidential election, and Viktor

Anpilov, the head of the far-left Communists. In addition, Zyuganov obtained the endorsement of former vice president Aleksandr Rutskoi, the leading Peronist among the nationalists, and Sergei Baburin, an important nationalist in the legislature. Thus he is going into the first round with only one other candidate on the Left, and he a regional candidate. Zyuganov is a heavy favorite to win the first round and is a virtual certainty to be one of the two candidates in the runoff.

Zyuganov has "won the primary" on the Left by emphasizing his desire to restore the Soviet Union in modified form. Under his control the Duma passed a nonbinding resolution declaring the dissolution of the USSR illegal. The resolution was timed to coincide with the fifth anniversary of the March 1991 referendum in which three-quarters of the population voted to preserve the Soviet Union. This referendum and a large Moscow meeting about it were not designed to have any real meaning, but merely to remind people that Yeltsin had overridden a strong majority in breaking up the USSR.

Zyuganov's emphasis on the decision to dissolve the Soviet Union has been meant to play upon an issue intimately connected with Yeltsin that three-quarters of the population strongly disapproved. The Communists did not emphasize nationalist issues in the 1993 Duma election, but after 1993 the issues proved a major weapon in capturing former supporters of Zhirinovsky and Lebed in December 1995. Zyuganov's reemphasis of them is now aimed at reducing support for the nationalists and making him the only oppositional alternative.

Zyuganov seems certain to be one of the candidates in the runoff, but the second candidate is more difficult to predict. With five other major candidates in the race, a small number of votes might be sufficient to allow a candidate to capture the second spot. If voters do vote strategically, they might do so in various ways. Yeltsin, as has been seen, has been far less sure-handed in projecting a political image. He seemed to move decisively toward the center and even the Left in the first months after the 1995 election, but then on substantive matters moved back toward the Right.

In March and early April, Yeltsin did everything possible to convince people that he could defeat Zyuganov in the runoff and that his second-place finish was inevitable. Yet if Yeltsin has made a rational political calculation in his retreat from his January and February move to the political center, then he is indicating real concern about the first round. He is acting as if his private polls suggest that the reform part of the spectrum might coalesce around Yavlinsky, Fedorov, or Lebed and that one of these might come in second if Yeltsin does not solidify his position on the Right.

Because Yavlinsky is so far to the Right and is so much a part of the young intellectual community that even Yeltsin, let alone the population, is rejecting, he seems like an unlikely candidate to stop Zyuganov. The most likely possibilities, then, are General Aleksandr Lebed or Svyatoslav Fedorov. There is also talk about a so-called Third Force alliance among the three, and it would make sense to have a team in which Lebed were the presidential candidate, Fedorov his proposed premier, and Yavlinsky his chief economist.

Leaving aside the problems of ego, and they are enormous, there are two obvious problems with this coalition. First, Fedorov and Yavlinsky would have little reason to trust Lebed if he were to win the presidency. They would have no political base from which to resist if he cast them aside. Second, a team in which Yavlinsky were in charge of economic reform would encounter resistance in the Duma unless he changed his approach drastically. In practical terms a Lebed-Yavlinsky alliance would almost surely represent the choice of a regime not unlike Pinochet's in Chile. Still, whatever its character, any such alliance would pose a powerful challenge to Yeltsin in the first round.

The problem for the other candidates is to create a political image, achieve significant name recognition, and establish themselves as the most likely stop-Zyuganov candidate. None has a meaningful political organization, and all must rely on television. But the television networks are hardly showing them, let alone giving them a chance to present their programs.

This is especially the case with Yeltsin's most dangerous opponent, General Aleksandr Lebed. With Lebed projecting the image of a Pinochet who will introduce order to permit capitalism to flourish, the most wealthy "new Russians" have every reason to finance him if they think he would be a stronger candidate against Zyuganov than Yeltsin and if they think campaign contributions will protect them from prosecution against corruption if he wins. If Lebed has a flood of effective television advertisements in the last month of the campaign, Yeltsin may be in the deepest of political trouble.

A series of questions arises. Will the new capitalists judge Lebed a stronger candidate than Yeltsin? Will they believe that contributing money to Lebed is safe? (In mid-April, it was reported that campaign contributions to Lebed or Yavlinsky would result in an immediate visit by the tax inspectors and confiscatory tax assessments.) Finally, if Yeltsin thinks he is losing, will he find a way to call off the election?

The senior author finds it difficult to believe in the ultimate likelihood of Yeltsin's election in July. The conditions of life for the average Russian are too terrible, the drop in agricultural production too precipitous, the decline in life expectancy too pronounced, Yeltsin's record of broken promises too complete, and his health too poor in a country with strong memories of Brezhnev's last years.

A Russian friend of the senior author buys milk in the countryside on the way home from his dacha. In early April he bought milk from a peasant who was drunk, and he asked if people in the countryside around Moscow were supporting Yeltsin. The peasant retorted with near indignation, "Who would vote for that drunkard?" If Yeltsin is too nonpresidential even for the drinking vote, the election may be over.

If the non-Communist electorate, rightly or wrongly, develops the same sense in the beginning of June, it is possible that support will shift massively away from Yeltsin to a stop-Zyuganov candidate. If the tax collectors believe Yeltsin is doomed, they will not harass businessmen and bankers contributing to other candidates. Those people working for the television networks will start worrying about the reaction of the next president, not the present one. Mancur Olson analyzed the collective action problems of autocrats in a way that is relevant for lame-duck presidents:

> If a government's operatives . . . *believe* that they will be punished if they fail to carry out their orders and rewarded if they do, an autocracy is secure. If the cadre perceive that a dictatorship is invincible, it cannot be overthrown by its subjects. Yet a regime whose power rests on nothing more than a shared perception can lose all of its power once perceptions change. And . . . perceptions can change in the blink of an eye. All the power of an imposing regime can vanish in the night air.[13]

This fact also needs to be taken into account by those advancing the hypothesis that Yeltsin will call off the election. The Communists are so well organized that they can easily put hundreds of thousands of people into the streets in protest. Military force could suppress these demonstrations, but the military is the one institution besides the Orthodox Church that is highly respected by the people and is very unlikely to want to support Yeltsin in such a situation.[14] According to highly detailed reports in extreme nationalist newspapers that were never meaningfully denied, Yeltsin tried to dissolve the Duma when it voted to annul the Belovezh decision to end the Soviet Union. The minister of the interior, Kulikov, refused to use his troops and resisted. Only the troops under the command of Yeltsin's personal security, Aleksandr Korzhakov, seem available for use,[15] and the professional military and security forces will surely not allow him to command the dominant troops in the country.

The one possibility worth considering arises if there are doubts about the election's outcome in the circles around Yeltsin. The Communists would probably renationalize the export industries, and they would be very much tempted to follow the example of South Korea and arrest former officials for corruption. If Yeltsin were removed from office before the election by whatever means, Premier Viktor Chernomyrdin would succeed him as president. The constitution says that a new election must be held in three months, and one can imagine the election being postponed for such a period to adjust the campaign to the new circumstances and to permit Chernomyrdin to organize his campaign.

Of course, the constitution says the premier is appointed by the president and confirmed by the Duma. Chernomyrdin's name was never submitted to the Duma, but only to the old dissolved Congress. It could be argued—and some in Moscow do—that Chernomyrdin is only the acting premier and, therefore, cannot succeed. They would say that the head of one of the two houses of parliament—Viktor Seleznev, chairman of the Duma, or Yegor Stroev, chairman of the Federation Council, would be the acting president. A major political crisis over the issue is fully possible, for there are good constitutional arguments on both sides of the issue. It is small wonder that all opposition candidates call for the establishment of legal order and that the respondents in our survey list it as the number one requirement in a democracy.

The Runoff

When we have discussed the strengths and weaknesses of the Communists, we have implicitly been discussing the runoff—a runoff in which Yeltsin is the other candidate. There is no need to repeat that analysis. On the surface it is easier to imagine how Zyuganov might win a landslide against Yeltsin than how he might lose.

Yet there are many imponderables. Zyuganov needs to move toward the center in a convincing manner, and he needs to get this message to an electorate without access to a free mass media. He has the dual problem of holding the core of his support—those strongly suspicious of economic reform—in the face of the challenge from Anpilov while gaining the more centrist voters he needs to achieve a majority. Zyuganov has every incentive to try to look presidential and to move toward the center. He can refer to Communist victories in Poland and Hungary as evidence that Communists are no longer inimical to the free market and democracy. But whether he can do this convincingly remains to be seen.

The raw figures suggest that a major breakthrough for the Communists in mass perceptions and a sweeping rejection of Boris Yeltsin occurred between 1993 and 1995, but only after the election will we know for certain the intensity of the rejection of Yeltsin and how comfortable a majority of the electorate is with the Communists, regardless of what they say.

The real question is the character of Russian political culture outside a few of the largest cities. The last two paragraphs, like the rest of this book, have treated the Russian electorate as a normal one that responds to political appeals in more or less the way a Western electorate would. Yeltsin obviously has the kind of record that, fairly or unfairly, would result in the defeat of any elected leader in the West. He seems in a worse position than Herbert Hoover in 1932 running against Franklin Roosevelt. Zyuganov, by contrast, seems to have all the right political instincts on how to position himself, form coalitions, and appeal to the ambiguous feelings of the population on issues such as Chechnia and the Union.

But is the electorate normal? Gavriil Popov, former mayor of Moscow, has argued that it is not. He sees Russians as having a traditional patriarchal attitude toward the tsar. So long as the tsar tosses out some "bad lieutenants," as he has done, shows he is the representative of the country in foreign policy, shows his good heart by promising everything to his subjects, and appeals emotionally for a second chance, the public will support him, especially against a man like Zyuganov who, in fact, seems not like a tsar but a modern politician.[16]

Popov shows the traditional contempt of Moscow intellectuals for workers in the big cities and others in the smaller cities and villages. It is, however, an electorate most of whose members have a high school diploma and one that has been very mistreated by Yeltsin's policy. Most elections for national leader tend to be a referendum on the incumbent. Russians, including most of those in the provinces, have had a long love affair with Boris Yeltsin, but in our view most of them want him out of their lives. They are not simply waiting for him to beg for forgiveness before they take him back.

If Yeltsin is not in the runoff, the character of the second candidate and the campaign he runs will be crucial. If Zhirinovsky were to make it to the second round, a broad coalition of reform and centrist forces would unite behind the Communists against him. If Lebed or Fedorov were to become a more effective candidate than he was in 1995 and come in second, either could be a formidable challenger to Zyuganov. So could Yavlinsky in conjunction with one of the others.

For a political scientist, the truly fascinating runoff would be between Lebed and Zyuganov. Lebed has the charismatic appeal of a tsar—a strong tsar—while Zyuganov creates the image of a normal Western president, although one whose capabilities and even programs are far from certain. Both appeal to anti-Western nationalism, but Lebed does so more convincingly than Zyuganov. Lebed also gives the impression of greater commitment to capitalist transformation than to social welfare, and he will strengthen this impression if he conducts a major television campaign financed by the new bourgeoisie.

Yet, as paradoxical as it seems, the Communist Zyuganov would be the candidate of democracy in a contest with Lebed. Barring some crisis at the end of the century, Zyuganov seems a man committed to working within a pluralist setting and cooperating with other elements of the political elite. The collective leadership tradition of the Communist party, honored more in the breach than in reality in the past, seems to have been internalized by Zyuganov, perhaps because he never rose high enough in the party apparatus to function in an independent way. Lebed's language is much more like Yeltsin's in treating the president as the embodiment of the public who is free to represent it as he sees fit. But if Yeltsin has not been repressive in exercising his rule, Lebed gives the impression of a man with very different instincts.

The central myth of the French Revolution was that liberty, equality, and fraternity all go together. The Russian Revolution of 1990–91 has been similar in seeing "reform" as indivisible. A Lebed-Zyuganov contest would highlight the inherent conflict between rapid marketization and the responsiveness to majority public opinion that is the essence of democracy. The supporters of the revolution would try to blur their choice with wishful thinking about one or another candidate, but ultimately they would have to make a choice. The senior author, rightly or wrongly, has long been convinced that the psychology of the Russians has changed fundamentally from the beginning of the century, that it has become essentially modern. Russians have seemed to prefer anarchy even to the normal use of force involved in a normal democracy, and it would be his hypothesis that the commitment of the majority to democracy remains strong. But, without question, a Zyuganov-Lebed race would provide a number of interesting tests of theory.

7

Conclusion

It is, of course, difficult to come to conclusions about the outcome of an election that has not taken place. This is particularly so because the election will scarcely be the end of political drama in Russia, regardless of the outcome. Zyuganov could be an ideal president if his policy corresponded with his most benign words, and if he succeeded in reconciling his followers to the new economic and political order. But he could become a horror if he followed the paths suggested by some of his supporters or simply proved incapable of solving the problems facing him. The outcome of victory by one of the other candidates, including Yeltsin, is no less unpredictable. A victorious president would have to deal with a legislature that is basically controlled by the Left and would have to choose between collaboration or confrontation with a party that is well organized and likely to feel it was cheated of the presidency.

The major surprise would occur if Yeltsin would fail to finish as one of the top two candidates in the first round of the presidential election. If Zhirinovsky or Yavlinsky were to finish second, either would seem a weak candidate in the second round against Zyuganov, and Zhirinovsky a hopelessly weak one. If Svyatoslav Fedorov or General Aleksandr Lebed were to catch fire and emerge in second place, either would be a much more formidable opponent.

A Yavlinsky, Fedorov, or Lebed presidency would face the problem encountered in even more intense form by a victorious Yeltsin—how to work with a Communist Duma. Fedorov might have a good working relationship and a fruitful policy, but Yavlinsky's instincts are close to Gaidar's, and he has been slow to reach beyond the academic community for associates and allies. He would have to modify his policy and approach greatly to avoid constant confrontation. To be an effective president, he would have to develop an organizational ability he has not yet shown.

General Lebed is the most unpredictable of the candidates. His weakness is his lack of a civilian organizational base, which would also make the character of his presidency hard to predict. His movement toward a more pro-market, more openly dictatorial stance only increases the uncertainity about his political position and about the policy he would follow as president. With the army behind him, Lebed is the one president who has a real chance of winning a confrontation with the Communist Duma in the streets. One could imagine his attempting a radical economic reform under authoritarian rule as did General Pinochet in Chile. Yet, his instincts seem far indeed from Moscow's Westernizers, and his associate, Sergei Glazev, has even been talking about close cooperation between Lebed and the Communists. Glazev certainly does not want a free trade policy, and his position—and that of Lebed—might be fairly close to that of the Duma. Lebed's lack of an organizational base gives him an incentive to work closely with the Communists in the Duma, but it is far from certain he would do this.

Because of the difficulty in describing the consequences of other candidates, this chapter will concentrate on the Yeltsin and Zyuganov alternatives—and more on Zyuganov because the Communists are more unknown and would be more likely to introduce major change. Nevertheless, the issues that are raised would be relevant not only if Zyuganov or Yeltsin were to win, but also someone else.

The Yeltsin Alternative

The consequences of a Yeltsin victory are more difficult to discuss than those of a Zyuganov victory. The West assumes that a Yeltsin victory would ensure continuity, but instead it would guarantee discontinuity with consequences that are very hard to predict. One cannot be sure what decisions Zyuganov would take, but it is fairly easy to analyze the choices he faces and to define the structure of his interests. By contrast, virtually everything is unknown about Yeltsin: the circumstances in which he would be elected, his relationship with the Communist-dominated Duma, the economic policy he would choose, and the state of his health.

The problems of analyzing a Yeltsin victory begin with the fact that his election would be considered illegitimate by the opposition and most of the people. Already the television coverage of the candidates is one-sided, and that includes the coverage on the "independent" television network. Any other irregularity would be emphasized, and a narrow Yeltsin victory—a landslide is inconceivable—would be attributed to fraudulent miscounting of the votes by

Yeltsin's administrative machinery. It does not matter whether such charges would be accurate; they would be widely believed, including by many who voted for Yeltsin.

Yeltsin has been following the same electoral strategy he followed before the June 1991 presidential election and the April 1993 referendum. He has been appropriating money for popular purposes (this time to pay off back wages), removing unpopular officials, slowing down privatization, and promising policy change in the direction the public wants. But at the same time he has been telling the International Monetary Fund he will raise oil prices toward market levels in July after the election, and his minions suggest to the West that the slowdown in privatization is a temporary election expedient. Already he has retreated on the tariff increases proposed by his finance minister in early March.[1]

If Yeltsin has been misleading the West rather than the Russian public, he may cohabit comfortably with the Communist-dominated Duma, for he has repeated most of the Communist program. Yet such a cohabitation would be totally out of character. He had every incentive to move to the center in December 1992 and January 1994, and even to remove Chernomyrdin after the humiliating defeat of Our Home Is Russia in December 1995. It is difficult to imagine why he would follow a different policy in 1996 and 1997 after he had won a presidential election he is certain to see as a referendum on his presidency.

Even if collaboration with the Duma were psychologically possible for Yeltsin, he would fear it for pragmatic reasons. If a new premier were to be appointed and confirmed by the Duma and if he introduced a change in policy that was successful, the premier would now get the credit, not Yeltsin. Since Russia does not have a vice president and the next person in the line of succession is the premier, Yeltsin would fear that the premier and the Duma would take advantage of his next bout of poor health to remove him from office.

Thus the most likely outcome of a Yeltsin victory would be a continuation of his present policy. A Communist majority in the Duma that believed it had been cheated in the presidential election would not be in a mood for the relatively nonconfrontational policy it has followed since the 1993 election. In a new confrontation, Yeltsin would almost surely see himself as he did in the first term—the embodiment of the people's will—and his instincts would lead him to try to deal with the Duma as he did with the Congress of People's Deputies.

"Unpredictable" is much too neutral a term to describe the outcome of a showdown between president and legislature. "Explosively unpredictable" is better. Neither Yeltsin nor the Congress had any significant popular support during their showdown in September 1993. The denouement was triggered by an insignificant and disorganized demonstration of a few thousand people who broke through an incompetently constructed police barrier. This time the Communist party has a well-functioning organization throughout the country, and both it and its followers would have real grievances. There would likely be massive demonstrations if Yeltsin tried to move against the Duma.

For Yeltsin to win in a showdown with the Duma, the military or security forces would have to go into the streets to quell demonstrations by a party whose anti-Westernism is closer to its heart than the policy of the president. At a number of points in the last six years, the military has had very good reasons to intervene in conflicts between civilians or simply to overthrow the civilian leadership, but it has not done so. It might intervene to support Lebed as president, but it is hard to imagine that it would change its nonintervention policy to support Yeltsin.

If the other civilian leaders agreed on a solution to a Yeltsin-Duma conflict, the problem might be solved easily, but because a showdown would be likely to occur over the person to be selected premier—the man in the succession and the extent of his authority—a constitutional solution would be hard to find. If the problem is to be solved unconstitutionally and the military is forced to intervene in the face of chaos, many scenarios are possible, some of them ugly.

The Zyuganov Alternative

It is easy to imagine various possibilities in the wake of a Yeltsin victory, but difficult to think of one outcome that is both probable and benign. By contrast, it is easy to think of several benign scenarios following a Zyuganov victory. Yeltsin's minister of the economy, Yevgeny Yasin, has said that "the threat of a Communist revanche is, naturally, very high. Why should it be any different here from Poland or Hungary?"[2] But if Zyuganov were, in fact, to be elected and were to follow the kind of social-democratic policy that the Communists are pursuing in Poland and Hungary, that would be an ideal outcome. Indeed, it is possible that Yasin was subtly trying to say that.

If Zyuganov were to introduce economic reform based on government-directed industrial investment, as have the Pacific Rim countries, and solve the problem of tax receipts by nationalizing the export industries (petroleum, natural gas, metal, and other natural resources), he would likely achieve a major economic turnaround. (Proponents of shock therapy insist one is imminent in any case.) He would provide the final legitimization and institutionalization of market reform and democracy by reconciling the great majority of the remaining skeptics to the new order.

Zyuganov is also ideally suited to introduce the agricultural reform that is absolutely vital for Russia. A program of free sale of land and dissolution of the collective farms would be extraordinarily foolish, and in fact radicals advance it only as a political cover for the current exploitive extraction of crops from peasants through the collective farm system. Even China leases agricultural land for fifteen years, and Russia needs to introduce reform in stages: first, autonomy for the collective farms with their managers free to produce and sell in response to market prices, then decentralization of decisionmaking power to subunits within the farm, and finally after some years, dissolution of the farm. Only in such a rational way can land be brought under the control not of uneducated peasants but of the millions of people with an agricultural college education and managerial experience who should be country's farmers.

The first step is price liberalization in agriculture, and the Yeltsin government (and Gorbachev's before him) have feared that such increases would cause political instability in the big cities. But Zyuganov has enough support in the countryside and among the urban poor to have a good chance of carrying through what will be a very delicate set of steps.

Similarly, the economic union that Zyuganov is proposing with the former republics of the Soviet Union theoretically has much to recommend it, at least if the Baltic republics are excluded. The economies of the republics are still integrated, they have industrial technologies not competitive with the West, and their elites have a similar education and know only Russian as a common language.[3] Countries such as England, France, and Germany have decided to abandon the sovereignty they had in 1939 and are moving toward economic integration with a common currency. It is hard to believe that Ukraine, Georgia, and Turkmenia will have the sovereignty of 1939 and that they too would not benefit from economic integration. They will not be ready for integration into the EEC for decades, but an eastern Common Market as an intermediate stage makes eminent economic sense.

But, of course, there are many questions about Zyuganov. First, as has been seen, Zyuganov's books and speeches contain frightening words as well as soothing ones. The Communist deputies in the Duma include men who are even more open in proclaiming an intention to carry out postelection measures that are truly alarming. Yeltsin and his supporters follow the familiar strategy of suggesting that each of the most extreme statements of Zyuganov and his most extreme supporters represent a secret Communist plan.

Large numbers of voters who are strongly anti-Yeltsin share these doubts about Zyuganov. If Russian voters trusted Zyuganov to be a Polish or Hungarian type of Communist, he obviously would receive 60 percent of the vote or more in a one-on-one contest with Yeltsin. With large segments of the Russian electorate being uncertain and suspicious (and with another large segment of Zyuganov's supporters holding truly frightening views), we too have every reason to be uncertain and suspicious.

We should not, however, frighten ourselves into believing that unfavorable results are necessarily certain or even probable. There is no evidence that Zyuganov is an ideological fanatic along the lines of Lenin, Stalin, Pol Pot, or even Viktor Anpilov, the leader of the rival Communist party in Russia. Lenin never went to Zurich to court foreign investments, nor did he pledge to support the Russian Orthodox Church as Zyuganov has. A fanatic misleads by employing words such as "democracy," "freedom," and "peace" in unfamiliar ways, but even then a careful reader can understand that sleight-of-hand is being used. Zyuganov is fairly concrete in the moderation he promises, and that is important.

But if Zyuganov is not a fanatic, it is important to understand his opportunities and his interests if he comes to power. The most unfortunate aspect of Yeltsin's constitution is that it will give Zyuganov ample opportunity to do virtually anything he wants. It was said at the time that the West was playing a dangerous game in supporting Yeltsin in his desire for an authoritarian constitution because it might be misused by his successor. That remains a danger. Zyuganov would have a majority in the Duma, and he would be commander-in-chief of the armed forces and could appoint the top generals. He has a program congenial to both the Duma and the military. The Federation Council is composed of the regional governors and chairmen of the regional legislatures, and they have no independent means of taxation to finance their activities. To get money from the Ministry of Finance in Moscow, the local officials must support Yeltsin, and in July they will support whoever is president for the same reason.

Some, of course, think that hard-line Communists will shove Zyuganov aside, and William Safire of the *New York Times* calls him a Kerensky—the transitional figure in 1917 whom Lenin replaced. Certainly there are some real hard-liners among the Communist deputies, but the alarmists say little about the scenarios in which Zyuganov would be removed.[4]

It is true that Zyuganov is subordinated to the Central Committee of the Communist party as party leader and that it could remove him from that post as the Soviet Central Committee removed Nikita Khrushchev in 1964. But it is not true that the party Central Committee could remove Zyuganov as Russian president. When the Soviet Central Committee was very angry at Gorbachev in 1990 and 1991, he always threatened to rule without it. The members of the

Central Committee understood they needed the president more than he needed them, and Zyuganov would be in the same position. Indeed there is no longer a significant Central Committee apparatus; the Communists rely on the staffs of their deputies in the Duma. The military could, of course, remove him, but he is likely to appoint a loyal defense minister. The military has been avoiding intervention in politics in the last six years despite some severe provocations and enormous temptations, and Zyuganov is likely to give them even less reason to intervene.

It is Zyuganov's apparent self-interests that lead to the most reassuring scenarios. The main problem for the alarmists is that he seems to have little personal incentive to follow the courses they hypothesize. For example, a victorious Zyuganov would have a guaranteed five-year term as president and a majority in the Duma. This gives him little incentive to abandon democracy quickly. A government structure in which the state governors and speakers of the state legislatures serve as part-time deputies in one house of the national legislature has little to recommend it, and one could imagine a crisis over its resistance to constitutional amendments. Yet the Communists have every reason to give priority to economic policy before they try to change the constitution in a way that requires immediate new elections.

Similarly, Zyuganov has a strong incentive to be very cautious about the reestablishment of the old Soviet Union. He is leader of the Russian Communist party and would be president of Russia. There is an all-Union Communist party with Oleg Shenin, a supporter of the 1991 coup d'etat, as its chairman and Yegor Ligachev as its deputy chairman. If the USSR were reestablished in a centralized form, Zyuganov's Russian Communist party would be subordinated to Shenin and Ligachev, and he as president would be less important than a USSR president. It is easy to believe Zyuganov will push hard for the economic union he proposes, but difficult to imagine he wants strong USSR institutions that will reduce his own power.

The most serious question about Zyuganov is his competence. He has shown great organizational ability in reconstructing the Communist party and in building a political coalition around it. In that sense he reminds a specialist on the Soviet Union of men such as Stalin and Brezhnev, who were underestimated because they were gray organizational men and lacked the ability and inclination to give fiery speeches.

Nevertheless, both Gorbachev and Yeltsin showed great sophistication and ability in gaining power and surprisingly little sophistication and ability in exercising it. They often ignored the most obvious political steps and strategies that would have benefited both themselves and their country. Zyuganov is a man who knows better how to operate in the new political environment, and he has a far greater understanding of the importance of institutions in human behavior than either Gorbachev or Yeltsin. Yet he has no experience in economics, and it remains to be seen whether he would govern more intelligently than Gorbachev or Yeltsin.

The West does not understand the scale of the problem faced by a Russian president. Both in the West and Russia, there has been a lot of lively ideological debate about economic reform, but it has centered on extraordinarily vague and largely irrelevant issues such as the free sale of land or macroeconomic policy. Only Zyuganov and his allies are talking about necessary changes in agricultural pricing; but no one, including Zyuganov, is presenting an intelligent or even intelligible strategy of any type for agricultural reform. Only Sergei Glazev is talking about the kind of export strategy that has worked so well in Asia. The reason for the vagueness seems not to be political coyness but a lack of knowledge about what to do, regardless of political orientation. There is little evidence that the policy community contains many people who understand the details of Chinese reform or the way Western corporations actually function, let alone the complex relationship between democracy and the market. Western advisers have given no help on any of these questions, but have only misled.

In the event of a Zyuganov victory the dangerous scenarios arise out of crises. In the near term most of these stem from relations with the former republics of the Soviet Union, notably Ukraine. Even if Zyuganov has the most benign intentions, nationalists are likely to interpret his every word and action as an attempt to reestablish the old order. Russian-language speakers are likely to have the opposite interpretation, and 40 percent of the urban people in Ukraine speak Russian as their native language. Confrontation is possible within the republics, especially Ukraine, and then the question will arise about what Russia will do. Nevertheless, in the long run a Russia that is beginning to grow economically has much to offer the non-Russian former republics. If Russia simply raises tariff barriers, the other former republics will have a compelling interest to come inside the tariff walls to maintain their natural market and to protect their technologically infant industries. Even the Baltic countries cannot ignore an economically vibrant St. Petersburg, which has more people than Estonia and Latvia combined and is only sixty miles from the Estonian border. Indeed, there will be those in eastern Europe who will bring up the desirability of some arrangement with Russia. Russia does not need to raise the question of political institutions. So long as the Russian bank and the Russian military have a dominant role, it will be other republics that will begin to call for supranational institutions to give themselves some control over these institutions.

In the longer run the problems for Zyuganov come in the economic realm. His greatest political problems will likely come not from the possibility of failure, but the probability of success. As the past six years have shown, economic depression gives most workers little leverage if they want to strike. It is when conditions start improving that unrest develops over perceived inequities in the division of the pie.

Moreover, in the short run, Zyuganov can solve the problem of tax shortfalls by nationalizing the industries that export petroleum, natural gas, and other raw materials. This will allow him to blame old leaders and businessmen for past failures and will give him resources to begin rebuilding the education and health systems. But of course, one of the reasons for the periodic patterns of privatization and renationalization in Asia and Latin America over the decades is to ensure that new rascals can gain control of resources that had been seized by old rascals.[5] Today the Yeltsin team is the *nomenklatura*, the center, against which resentment is directed; tomorrow it will be the *nomenklatura* associated with any new president.

The American Response

American newspapers have been carrying a debate as to whether the Communists can be trusted to have an essentially social-democratic domestic policy and a relatively benign foreign policy. To some extent this debate is a surrogate for a quieter debate as to whether the United States should encourage Yeltsin to call off the election if the Communists seem likely to win. The debate is also preparation for a U.S. presidential campaign that could turn on whether Bill Clinton "lost Russia" if the Communists win. And of course, to a considerable extent the debates reflect genuine uncertainty about the outcome if Zyuganov comes to power.

Because the Communist's ability to organize demonstrations makes any attempt to call off the election problematic, the United States should be concentrating on its response to the postelection situation. The situation in Russia is certain to change, either because of a new president or because of a confrontation between the president and the Duma. A United States that either directly or through the IMF simply pushes old formulas will be irrelevant at best.

The debate on Russia should not become a partisan issue. There has been an amazing consensus on the essence of policy under both the Bush and Clinton administrations. In the geostrategic realm the "strategic partnership" of the Clinton administration has been an unacknowledged continuation of the "Vladivostok to Vancouver" policy of the Bush administration.[6] And whatever the instincts of the Bush administration about stability, it followed the Western media in praising the enthusiasm of the Moscow revolutionaries for a de facto shock therapy in economic matters. Just as the Clinton administration can be severely criticized for its support of Yegor Gaidar and his policy long after it had failed economically and politically, so one of the last acts of George Bush as president was to call Boris Yeltsin and ask him to fight for the retention of Gaidar as premier in December 1992.[7]

There has been across the American political spectrum an extraordinarily strange dichotomy in thinking about Russia and China. The Chinese economic transformation is seen as a near miracle, and in fact it has produced great structural change and a growth rate of 10 percent a year at the same time. While the American president and the press worried about $500 million sales of American chicken to Russia, the New York Times reported that foreign companies had invested $340 billion in China in the last four years.[8]

Similarly, American newspapers insisted Yeltsin's economic reform was successful because inflation was declining to 3 percent a *month* and a Communist victory would heat up inflation. Yet, they reported that China had decided to cut its growth from 10.2 percent in 1995 to a mere 8 percent in 1996 in order to cut its inflation from 14.8 percent a *year* to 10 percent.[9] Then on May 1, 1996, the New York Times reported that, in fact, the Chinese economy had grown by 10.2 percent in the first quarter while inflation dropped to 7.7 percent. Hence China was able to cut interest rates. On the same day, an editorial in the newspaper pleaded with Yavlinsky not to join with Lebed because the general wants a more managed economy.[10]

Yet everyone knows China is far from adopting a modern capitalist system or even an overregulated capitalist system such as exists in India. Everyone knows that China has taken nearly twenty years to reach even this point in its reform. Everyone knows China in 1978 was less than thirty years from its revolution and had a whole generation of middle-aged officials with personal experience of a capitalist economy as well as millions of overseas Chinese eager to support reform in the old country. And sophisticated observers also knew that the authoritarian Chinese political system has made economic transformation simpler to achieve.

No one of significance in Russia still remembers the pre-1917 economic system, and Russia has no large overseas Russian community to help. The democratic institutions have obviously made it more difficult to resist populist pressures. Yet Russia is supposed to leap across a chasm in 500 days that China has not succeeded in crossing in twenty years. Indeed, it is said that a transition of twenty years' length would be impossible in Russia. Gorbachev and Yeltsin are berated for not achieving the impossible.

The West desperately needs to gain some historical perspective and to reflect on its centuries-old experience and that of countries such as Japan and Brazil in introducing democracy and capitalism. It was an experience in which countries such as Germany, Italy, and Spain were afflicted with fascist regimes after experience with democracy, sometimes with disastrous consequences for foreign policy. Foreign economic policy was a key element in these political transformations, with free trade often having explosive political consequences.[11]

There is a vast literature reflecting the world's accumulated thought about the relationship between politics and economics. For centuries political analysts and philosophers have explored the dilemmas and internal contradictions of democracy as a form of government—in particular the problem that a modern market needs predictability and the protection of, in John Locke's words, "life, liberty, and property." The great dilemma of the modern political system is how to ensure enough predictability and freedom of capitalist enterprise within a market system without denying people the democratic opportunity to decide on the most crucial questions affecting their lives. But if a government can be installed on the basis of a vote of 51 percent of the people, a surge of popular emotion or despair may bring to power outsiders who destroy the predictability on which a market rests. The conservatives in the nineteenth century who denounced democracy as mob rule or the U.S. Founding Fathers who were concerned with the tyranny of the majority and instituted checks and balances against it were reacting to a very real danger.

It is for this reason that the West has abandoned any attempt to introduce pure democracy, but instead has chosen constitutional democracy. The essence of constitutional democracy is the imposition of limitations on the majority and its representatives and the refusal to allow the majority the right to pass laws on certain subjects. The expansion of the role of the U.S. government during the New Deal and the later conflict over states' rights and segregation led to a most sophisticated discussion about the dilemmas of federalism, the conflict between majority rights and minority rights, and the relationship of government regulation and property rights. It is a discussion Americans need to reread. The tortured history of changing U.S. Supreme Court decisions on segregation, the due process clause, and abortion shows that the line between the permissible and impermissible in a constitutional democracy is neither easy to define nor permanently fixed. But the fact that these decisions are made by an unelected Supreme Court whose judges have life tenure is the surest sign of the limitations on democracy.

A very large proportion of people's political struggle in all countries focuses on efforts to obtain more than the market would provide or limit the harmful effects of the market on themselves: this includes efforts to obtain subsidies or contracts, legalize trade unions, establish zoning laws, limit hours and child labor, prohibit the sale of goods and services (that is, narcotics and prostitution), limit the risk of personal individual investment by giving corporations the status of legal individuals, raise or lower interest rates, achieve various goals by restructuring the tax code, constrict the labor market by establishing professional requirements and licensing, institute tariffs and import quotas, and regulate harm to the environment. The frequent success of such efforts is the reason capitalist economies used to be called *mixed economies*, and that term is really more accurate than *capitalism*. The essence of democracy—indeed, to a large extent its purpose—is to ensure that the population can protect itself against the workings of a pure market.

Those who dominated American policy toward Russia—they have mostly been economists—talked only about the immediate introduction of market prices, tight money, free trade, freedom to the enterprise, the end of all subsidies, and democracy (not constitutional democracy). Yet everyone knows that the corporation gives no autonomy to the assembly plant, that Saudi Arabia produces petroleum effectively with its nationalized industry, that the Pacific Rim countries have grown rapidly despite their protectionism, and that China is considered a stunning example of successful economic reform and certainly of penetration into the world market despite its many deviations from the pure market model. Everyone knows that the relationship of politics and economic policy is almost always different in earlier stages of industrialization and democratic development than at later ones and that freer trade is generally introduced (as it is now in Japan) only when a society reaches a stage in which the consumer rather than the producer becomes dominant.

This is not the time for lectures to Gennady Zyuganov, if he becomes president, on these matters, although it is time for lectures to Boris Yeltsin if he does. It is, however, a time for realism in adjusting to decisions that would be taken in Russia. Capitalism has many forms, and we live comfortably with those in the Pacific Rim, in Sweden, in Saudi Arabia, and so forth. We cannot judge Russia and only Russia by the standards of the most doctrinaire ideological models. We cannot give advice only on the basis of these models instead of more sophisticated advice on how best to achieve the mixed economies found in the modern world.

When the Communists ruled the Soviet Union in the past, we were extremely sensitive to the fact that only that country had the nuclear capability of destroying the United States. We have become insensitive to that fact, and we need to return to the insights of the past whether the Communists return to power or not. We have been taking terrible chances in our policy toward Russia—the chance that some anti-Western totalitarian will come to power, the chance that control will be lost over nuclear stockpiles and that nuclear weapons will fall into the hands of terrorists. In a world in which the most likely adversary of the twenty-first century will be one of the Asian countries with more than a billion people, there is not even a geopolitical reason to take this chance, but every geopolitical reason to ensure that Russia has a stable government and prosperous society. America is renowned for its pragmatism. The time has come for the pragmatists to retake control over policy toward Russia.

Notes

Chapter 1

1. In fact Zhirinovsky often supported the Chernomyrdin government on important matters.

2. In addition to the MacArthur Foundation, this work was financed by the Carnegie Corporation, the National Science Foundation (SBR-94-02548 and SBR-94-12051), and the Brookings Institution. Timothy Colton was co-PI on this study. He and Jerry Hough are coediting a detailed study of the 1993 election, *Proto-Democracy in Russia*, that will be published by Brookings.

3. The PIs on this study, which was financed by the National Science Foundation (SBR-92-12332), were David Laitin of the University of Chicago and Jerry Hough, with Susan Lehmann participating informally. The former republics of the Soviet Union were Estonia, Kazakhstan, Latvia, and Ukraine; the former Russian republics were Bashkortostan and Tatarstan. Guboglo supervises the network in the republics and was solely responsible for this work in Moscow.

4. This study, with Hough, Lehmann, and Ralph Clem of Florida International University as PIs, was financed by the U.S. State Department.

5. This study was funded by the National Science Foundation (SBR-96-00413) with the assistance of the U.S. Information Agency. The study was conducted under the auspices of the Brookings Institution.

6. As will be discussed later, nomenclature is a real problem in discussing Russia. In analysis of events in 1995 we will use the language of that time—right wing to denote strong support of market forces and left wing to denote Communists. In 1990, however, the word *conservative* denoted those who were resistant to change, and we will use it in the early discussion in that sense to mean left-wing, not the free-market conservatism of the Margaret Thatcher or Ronald Reagan type.

7. For the 1993 election, see Jerry F. Hough, "The Russian Election of 1993: Public Attitude toward Economic Reform and Democratization," *Post-Soviet Affairs*, vol. 10, no. 1 (1994), pp. 1–37.

8. Ralph S. Clem and Peter R. Craumer, "A Rayon-Level Analysis of the Russian Election and Constitutional Plebiscite of December 1993," *Post-Soviet Geography*, vol. 36, no. 8 (1995), pp. 459–75. The result about distance from oblast capital has been reported to the authors in a private communication.

9. Regina Smyth, "Ideological vs. Regional Cleavages: Do Radicals Control the RSFSR Parliament?" *Journal of Soviet Nationalities*, vol. 1 (Fall 1990), pp. 112–57; Ralph S. Clem and Peter R. Craumer, "The Geography of the April 25, 1993, Russian Referendum," *Post-Soviet Geography*, vol. 34, no. 8 (1993), pp. 481–96; Darrell Slider, Vladimir Gimpelson and Sergei Chugrov, "Political Tendencies in Russia's Regions: Evidence from the 1993 Parliamentary Elections," *Slavic Review* (1994), pp. 711–32; and Evelyn Davidheiser, "Region, Sector, Class in the 1993 Russian Parliamentary Election," paper presented at the 1994 annual meeting of the American Political Science Association.

10. The question used is: "Now I will list the parties and blocs who are nominating their candidates to the Federal Assembly. Which of them do you know? How do you react to those you know?" The answers were "positive," "more positive than negative," "more negative than positive," and "negative." In both tables, those without an opinion about Communists are excluded.

11. Clifford Gaddy, *The Price of the Past: Russia's Struggle with the Legacy of a Militarized Economy* (Brookings, 1996).

12. Linda J. Cook, *The Soviet Social Contract and Why It Failed: Welfare Policy and Workers' Politics from Brezhnev to Yeltsin* (Harvard University Press, 1993), pp. 1–2.

13. Michigan is not atypical in having its economic center in Detroit, its capital in Lansing, and its great university in Ann Arbor.

14. For an op-ed article that provided statements on the subject by a range of Republican presidents, see Alfred E. Eckes, "Who Says Republicans Are Free Traders?" *New York Times*, February 27, 1996, p. 23.

15. The nineteenth century Slavophiles in Russia were also for free trade because they hoped foreign competition would be so harmful to the country's infant industry that industry would remain small.

16. The previous pages are summarized from Evelyn Davidheiser, *The Paradox of Russian Politics: Economic Transformation under Tsars and Presidents* (forthcoming).

17. Alex Inkeles and David H. Smith, *Becoming Modern: Individual Change in Six Developing Countries* (Harvard University Press, 1974).

18. Robert Putnam, *Making Democracy Work* (Princeton University Press, 1993).

19. Except in the case of Novosibirsk, few distinguished between the largest provincial cities and the lesser ones. The problem was that the largest cities were defense cities and often closed to Westerners. Thus, Sakharov's exile to Gorki (now Nizhne Novgorod) was treated as banishment to the wilderness, but Gorki was Russia's third largest city and, it turned out in 1989 and 1990, quite liberal in its voting behavior.

20. See Yegor Gaidar's published doctoral dissertation, *Ekonomicheskie reformy i*

ierarkhicheskie struktury (Moscow: Nauka, 1990). The argument explicitly rested on Mancur Olson, *The Rise and Decline of Nations: Economic Growth, Stagflation, and Social Rigidities* (Yale University Press, 1982). See also Anders Aslund, *How Russia Became a Market Economy* (Brookings, 1995), p. 8.

21. This wildly utopian plan was authored by Grigory Yavlinsky, the founder of the Yabloko party.

22. Edward D. Mansfield and Jack Snyder, "Democratization and the Danger of War," *International Security*, vol. 20 (Summer 1995), pp. 5–38. For further discussion of the issue see "Correspondence: Democratization and the Danger of War," *International Security*, vol. 20 (Spring 1996), pp. 176–207.

23. Paradoxically, the young mathematical economists in Moscow found the work of modern neoclassical economists congenial because they had learned their economics from Karl Marx, who was himself analyzing the same precorporate nineteenth century capitalism as were the classical economists.

24. Foreign Broadcast Information Service, *Daily Report: Central Eurasia*, February 20, 1996, supplement, p. 1.

Chapter 2

1. This is analyzed at length in Jerry F. Hough, *Democratization and Revolution in the U.S.S.R, 1985-1991* (Brookings, 1996). This chapter draws much of its material from that book.

2. The key difference was in the freedom of the nominating process. The average number of candidates in Russian territorial districts rose from 1.98 in the 1989 election to 6.3 in 1990. Even electoral districts in which the largest town or village contained less than 100,000 people had 4.8 candidates on average compared with 1.6 in 1989. In addition, politicians had more time to prepare for the 1990 election and had learned from their experiences in 1989.

3. Boris Yeltsin, *The Struggle for Russia* (Random House, 1994), p. 157.

4. Susan Goodrich Lehmann, "Costs and Opportunities of Marketization: An Analysis of Russian Employment and Unemployment," in Richard L. Simpson and Ida Harper Simpson, eds., *Research in the Sociology of Work,* vol. 5: *The Meaning of Work* (Greenwich, Conn.: JAI Press, 1995), pp. 205–34.

5. Mancur Olson, *The Rise and Decline of Nations: Economic Growth, Stagflation, and Social Rigidities* (Yale University Press, 1982).

6. It remains very unclear who actually developed the policy. The obvious candidate was Aleksandr Shokhin, Gaidar's closest associate at first and the deputy premier in charge of the social sphere. In a private interview, however, he denied responsibility and treated the policy as something that evolved spontaneously. Gaddy treats it as a policy virtually forced upon the government as a fait accompli by managers who continued to

produce without orders and dared the government not to pay wages. Clifford Gaddy, *The Price of the Past: Russia's Struggle with the Legacy of a Militarized Economy* (Brookings 1996).

7. Martin Wolf, "Soviet Banker with Revolutionary Ideas," *Financial Times*, March 22, 1990, p. 23.

8. *Izvestiia*, February 10, 1993, 9. 1. In this respect Yeltsin followed tsarist practice. Witte kept the ordinary budget always in balance to encourage foreign investment, but the secret budget consistently ran a deficit.

9. The income data come from our survey. There is, of course, a small segment of the population in the private and even criminal sectors who would not report their incomes accurately—and probably do not agree to be interviewed by sociologists. The use of data on salary from a person's basic job avoids the problem of the second income, where misreporting to avoid taxes is frequent. But the high unreported incomes are almost surely made by people in groups already reporting higher income, and thus greater accuracy would only emphasize the point.

10. Radio Rossii, December 1, 1991 in Foreign Broadcast Information Service, *Daily Report: Russia*, December 2, 1991, p. 4.

11. Laws could be passed by the Congress only by a majority of all deputies, not a majority of all present, and attendance was often a problem. Similarly, constitutional amendments or impeachment required two-thirds of all deputies. Absences and abstentions therefore counted as a negative vote in both types of balloting. Although the vote for Yeltsin's impeachment seems at first glance much more substantial than that taking away his emergency powers, it was actually marginally lower. The only figures that mattered were the 623 votes to end the emergency powers and the 617 votes to impeach, not the 382 and 269 votes against.

12. *Rossiiskaia Gazeta*, May 19, 1993, pp. 2–3. However, the electoral commission included spoiled ballots in the denominator and thus reduced the reported favorable vote by several percentage points.

Chapter 3

1. These figures are based on interviews in the last five days of the campaign from a 35,000-respondent unweighted sample.

2. Each region, even ones with small populations, received at least one deputy, and this introduced great variance into the population of the districts. The districts in larger regions varied more than in 1990 because there were only one-quarter as many districts. However, the use of electors (adult citizens) rather than the entire population does discriminate against regions with larger numbers of children. This had a significant impact in 1993.

3. The Federation Council election is not important for the purposes of this book, for it usually was nonpartisan. Appointed officials in the executive, ultimately subordinate

to Yeltsin himself, comprised 55 percent of the deputies elected. In 1995 the deputies were, in fact, selected as originally intended.

4. See Jerry F. Hough "Institutional Change and the 1993 Election Results," in Timothy Colton and Jerry F. Hough, eds., *Proto-Democracy in Russia* (Brookings, forthcoming).

5. Khasbulatov and Rutskoi may have made a serious mistake in taking their resistance to Yeltsin's dissolution of the Congress so far. If the Chechen Khasbulatov had formed a republic-based party and Rutskoi a moderate nationalist one, with both seizing the banner of democracy in their fight against Gaidar, they likely would have done extremely well, and the composition of the Duma would have looked very different.

6. Before the 1995 election, the leadership of Women of Russia moved sharply toward the right (that is, in a pro-Yeltsin direction). As a consequence, its share of the vote shrank to 4.7 percent in the election, and it failed to achieve any representation.

7. For example, a rapid increase in the production of an item usually lowers its price in the West. Over time its contribution to the increase in gross domestic product measured in dollars is not as great as the percentage increase of the physical units. In the Soviet Union, pricing tended to be cost-plus; increases in the physical production of items tended to be translated into comparable increases in their monetary value.

8. *Ekonomika i zhizn'*, no. 1 (1996), p. 1.

Chapter 4

1. Jeffrey Sachs, "Komu grozit korrumpovannaia Rossiia," *Moskovskie novosti*, December 24, 1995, p. 7.

2. David Hoffman, "Pre-election Pause in Privatization," *Washington Post*, March 30, 1996, p. 12.

3. Those with this view split their party vote in line with the national average. It was those who chose people's power who most supported the Left and those who chose individual freedom or private property who most strongly supported the Right.

4. We often forget that the name of the Nazi party, even though it opposed nationalization and communism, was an abbreviation for National Socialist party.

5. Ralph S. Clem and Peter R. Craumer, "The Geography of the 1995 Russian Parliamentary Election: Continuity, Change, and Correlates," *Post-Soviet Geography*, vol. 36, no. 10 (1995), pp. 587–615.

6. The figures are from *Biuleten' Tsentral'noi Izbiratel'noi Komissii Rossiiskoi Federatsii*, no. 1 (1994), pp. 38, 67. There were also unproven allegations of fraud, some of them fairly implausible. However, local officials were under severe pressure to report high turnout on the referendum, but they may have been more than eager to find a reason to find something to invalidate a party list ballot cast for the "wrong" party.

7. *Rossiiskaia gazeta* (special edition), January 24, 1996, p. 2, provides the party breakdown for the country as a whole and for each region.

8. In practice, some persons elected with one party's endorsement defected to another

faction. Thus, five communists joined the People's Power faction and six the Agrarians, apparently for tactical political reasons to solidify the alliance among them.

9. In 1993 the Asiatic oblasts, most of which are below the fifty-fifth degree latitude that usually defines the upper limit of the south, had voted like the European north, but in 1995 they shifted in a conservative direction. Clem and Craumer, "Geography of the Russian 1995 Parliamentary Election," p. 596.

Chapter 5

1. Kevin Fedarko, "Yeltsin's Secret Report on How to Call Off the Vote," *Time*, April 8, 1986, pp. 38–39.

2. The election rules state that a runoff must be held within fifteen days after the count is completed, and Russia has a long tradition of Sunday elections. If there is a clear gap between the second- and third-place finishers, it should be easy to obtain an official count within a week. If a recount is needed, the runoff election could be pushed back.

3. Fred Hiott, "Ex-Aides Raise Questions about Yeltsin's Drinking," *Washington Post,* October 8, 1994, p. 21.

4. Korzhakov was a figure of significance as early as 1991. See Aleksandr Lebed, *Za devchavu obidno* (Moscow: Moskovskaia pravda, 1995), pp. 386–96.

5. *Izvestiia*, February 6, 1996, p. 3.

6. Michael R. Gordon, "Russia Agrees to Closer Links with Three Ex-Soviet Lands, *New York Times*, March 30, 1996, p. 4.

7. David Hoffman, "Pre-Election Pause in Privatization," *Washington Post*, March 30, 1996, p. 12.

8. Steve Liesman, "Some Russian Officials Are Moving to Reverse Business Privatization," *Wall Street Journal*, March 20, 1996, p. 1.

9. Chrystia Freeland, "Russia's Future Played Out in Steel Mill," *Financial Times*, March 4, 1996, p. 2.

10. Dimitri K. Simes, "Get Ready for a New Russia," *Washington Post*, April 7, 1996, "Outlook" sec., p. 1.

11. Michael Hudson, "Yeltsin's Land Decree Is Illegal and Risky," *New York Times*, March 20, 1996. p. 18.

12. For all the fanfare about the size of its commitment, the IMF awarded the Russian government $6.6 billion in April 1995 for the coming year, $550 million a month. The new tentative commitment is $300 million a month. In the name of helping Yeltsin the IMF was cutting back support. Chrystia Freeland, "IMF Strikes Hard Bargain with Moscow," *Financial Times*, February 24–25, 1996, p. 2; and Richard W. Stevenson, "Did Yeltsin Get a Sweetheart Deal on I.M.F. Loans?" *New York Times*, March 11, 1996, p. 11.

13. Michael R. Gordon, "Russia Drops Big Tariff Increase, Clearing Way for an IMF Loan," *New York Times*, March 26, 1996, p. 1.

14. NTV television, February 23, 1996, in Foreign Broadcast Information Service, *Daily Report: Central Eurasia*, February 26, 1996, pp. 25–26.

15. The obkom party secretary for agriculture from 1973 to 1984 was Yegor Stroev, who then became oblast party first secretary of the Orel oblast from 1985 to 1990. He was the last Central Committee secretary for agriculture under Gorbachev and, as governor of Orel, was elected chairman of the Federation Council in March 1996. It is said Stroev is associated with Our Home Is Russia and is loyal to Yeltsin, but an outsider can be permitted to wonder. Stroev takes care to emphasize his good relations with all candidates, but especially Zyuganov.

16. Here, as elsewhere, the best biographical directory is *Kto est' Kto v Rossii i v blizhnem zarubezh'e: Spravochnik* (Moscow: Vse dlia bas, 1993). Zyuganov's biography is on pp. 262–63.

17. Alessandra Stanley, "On Russia's Campaign Trail, Communist Recasts the Past," *New York Times*, March 27, 1996, p. 1; and Lee Hockstader, "Russian Communist Is Talking Tough," *Washington Post*, April 10, 1996, p. 1.

18. Stephen F. Cohen, "If Not Yeltsin: Four Voices of the Russian Opposition," *Washington Post*, December 3, 1995, "Outlook" sec., p. 3; and Craig R. Whitney, "Soothing Tone by Russian Communist at Business Forum," *New York Times*, February 5, 1996, p. 1.

19. The reader who wants a sense of just how moderate and reassuring Zyuganov is trying to be should look at the transcript of his interview on NTV television immediately after the Communists nominated him for president. NTV, February 16, 1996, in FBIS, *Daily Report: Central Eurasia*, February 22, 1996, p. 21; and Alessandra Stanley, "Russian Communist Aims for Broad Appeal," *New York Times*, March 18, 1996, p. 9.

20. David Hoffman, "Russia's Communists: How Far Can They Go?" *Washington Post*, February 26, 1996, p. 12.

21. ITAR-TASS, February 21, 1996, in FBIS, *Daily Report: Central Eurasia*, February 23, 1996, p. 19.

22. ITAR-TASS, March 27, 1996, in FBIS, *Daily Report: Central Eurasia*, March 27, 1996.

23. *Sovetskaia Rossiia*, March 19, 1996, p. 2.

24. Interfax, March 29, 1996, in FBIS, *Daily Report: Central Eurasia*, April 1, 1996, p. 3.

25. *Sovetskaia Rossiia*, March 19, 1996, p. 2. Yeltsin has been reluctant to allow elected governors where a governor is currently supporting him and might lose.

26. Alessandra Stanley, "Russia's Press Edits Out a Communist," *New York Times*, March 31, 1996, sec. 4, p. 4.

27. Interfax, January 25, 1996, in FBIS, *Daily Report: Central Eurasia*, January 26, 1996, p. 17.

28. See Jerry F. Hough, *Struggle for the Third World: Soviet Debates and American Options* (Brookings, 1985). A more accurate title for this book would be *Prelude to*

Perestroika, for it analyzes the debates through which Soviet scholars attacked and undermined Marxist-Leninist orthodoxy.

29. Gennady Zyuganov, *Derzhava* (Moscow: Informpechat, 1994), pp. 86–88. For some of his more extreme nationalist statements, see Andrian Karatynychy, "The Real Zyuganov," *New York Times,* March 5, 1996, p. 23.

30. *Obshchaia gazeta,* no. 11 (March 21–27, 1996), p. 8.

31. Zyuganov, *Derzhava,* pp. 90–91.

32. *Kommersant-Daily,* March 6, 1996, p. 3.

33. WPROST (Poznan), in FBIS, *Daily Report: Central Eurasia,* January 3, 1996, p. 8.

34. *Trud-7,* March 7–15, 1996, p. 5.

35. Public television, March 15, 1996, in FBIS, *Daily Report: Central Eurasia,* March 18, 1996, pp. 16–17.

36. Richard B. Dobson, "Russians—Disillusion Deepens," *USIA Opinion Analysis,* M-105-95, July 12, 1995; and Richard B. Dobson, "Russians Remain Dissatisfied as Parliamentary Election Draws Near," *USIA Opinion Alert,* L-67-95, November 9, 1995.

37. For an article very categorical in its accusations about Skokov, see *Nezavisimaia gazeta,* February 28, 1996, p. 1.

38. Lebed, *Za devchavu obidno,* pp. 320–28. Indeed, he describes his personal challenge to Yakovlev on the floor of the Twenty-Eighth Party Congress in 1990.

39. *Rabochaia tribuna,* April 23, 1996, p. 2.

40. *Sobesednik,* no. 10, March 1996, p. 3; *Komsomol'skaia pravda,* March 19, 1996, p. 3. These can be read in FBIS, *Daily Report: Central Eurasia,* March 22, 1996, pp. 23–26, and March 28, 1996, pp. 25–28.

41. Cohen, "If Not Yeltsin," p. 3.

42. *Komsomol'skaia pravda,* March 19, 1996, p. 2.

43. April 3, 1996, p. 2.

44. *Nezavisimaia gazeta,* December 21, 1995, p. 9.

45. Boris Fedorov resigned as Yeltsin's minister of finance a month later over the same issue.

46. As late as March 27, 1996, the respected newspaper *Kommersant Daily* could still say that "the electoral program of Yavlinsky himself is still a closely guarded secret" (p. 3).

Chapter 6

1. NTV television, January 28, 1996, in Foreign Broadcast Information Service, *Daily Report: Central Eurasia,* January 29, 1996, p. 20.

2. Lee Hockstader, "Yeltsin's Rough Campaign Is Paved with Promises," *Washington Post,* April 6, 1996, p. 13; and Alessandra Stanley, "Spendthrift Candidate Yeltsin: Miles to Go, Promises to Keep," *New York Times,* May 4, 1996, p. 1.

3. Oleg Savelev, "Chislo aktivnykh izbiratelei stabil'no rastet," *Segodnia*, March 21, 1996, p. 3.

4. NTV television, March 31, 1996 in FBIS, *Daily Report: Central Eurasia*, April 1, 1996, p. 23.

5. This decline occurred despite the extensive media coverage that Yabloko received just as the ballot was being finalized, when the Central Election Commission ruled to exclude the party for violating the rules about listing candidates. There was a tremendous uproar, Yabloko was reinstated within a week, and it came out of the incident better off for the press coverage it had received.

6. Michael Specter, "Yeltsin's Good Week: He's Back in the Race," *New York Times*, April 7, 1996, p. 1; and Lee Hockstader, "Yeltsin Finds a Reelection Strategy—and Campaign Message," *Washington Post*, April 7, 1996, p. 1.

7. "U chitalei 'AEF' vybory Presidenta uzhe nachalas," *Argumenty i fakty*, no. 16 (April 1996), p. 2.

8. We are grateful to Sergei Tumanov of Moscow University for these data.

9. *Demograficheskii ezhegodnik Rossiiskoi Federatsii, 1993* (Moscow: Goskomstat, 1994), p. 84; and "Goskomstat *Rossiia*," *Informatsionnyi statisticheskii biulletien*, no. 5 (May 1995), p. 35.

10. *Naselenie SSSR 1987: Statisticheskii sbornik* (Moscow: Finansy i statistiki, 1988), p. 5.

11. *Demograficheskii ezhegodnik Rossiiskoi Federatsii, 1993*, p. 94; and *The American Almanac 1995–1996: Statistical Abstract of the United States* (Austin, Tex.: Reference Press, 1995), p. 87.

12. Alessandra Stanley, "Russia's Press Edits Out a Communist, *New York Times*, March 31, 1996, sec. 4, p. 1; and Lee Hockstader, "Russian Media Stack the Deck for Yeltsin," *Washington Post*, April 3, 1996, p. 1.

13. Mancur Olson, "The Logic of Collective Action in Soviet-Type Societies," *Journal of Soviet Nationalities*, vol. 1 (Summer 1990), pp. 16–17.

14. In our survey, 52 percent expressed trust in the Russian Orthodox Church and 16 percent distrust, and 51 percent and 25 percent respectively in the military. Thirteen percent expressed trust in the presidential administration, 16 percent in the Duma, and 20 percent in the Ministry of Foreign Affairs.

15. Korzhakov indeed wants to call off the election. Michael Specter, "Aide to Yeltsin Calls for Delay in June Election," *New York Times*, May 6, 1996, p. 1.

16. *Argumety i Fakty*, no. 8 (1996), p. 3.

Chapter 7

1. Michael Gordon, "Russia Drops Big Tariff Increase, Clearing Way for an I. M. F. Loan," *New York Times*, March 26, 1996, p. 1.

2. Chrystia Freeland, "Last Reformer in the Kremlin Fights On," *Financial Times*, March 18, 1996, p. 3.

3. One usually talks about the Russian language in the non-Russian republics in terms of Russification, but Georgians, Armenians, and Azerbaidzhani in the Transcaucasus, for example, cannot understand each other's language. It will take decades before they learn a new international language such as English, and Russian will have to be their main language in interrepublican economic and political relations.

4. The hard-liners include General Makashev, who was one of the strongest reactionaries at the end of the Gorbachev period and commanded the mob that stormed the central television studios during the confrontation between the Congress and president in 1993. General Varennikov participated in the August 1991 coup and openly accuses top Gorbachev aides of being CIA spies in his memoirs.

5. Amy L. Chua, "The Privatization-Nationalization Cyle: The Link between Markets and Ethnicity in Developing Countries," *Columbia Law Review* (March 1995).

6. See, for example, Strobe Talbott, "Terms of Engagement," *New York Times*, February 4, 1996, sec. 4, p. 13, especially his emphasis on "undivided Europe."

7. Boris Yeltsin, *The Struggle for Russia* (Times Books, 1996), p. 199.

8. Sandra Sugawara, "China Market Set to Elipse Its Neighbors, *New York Times*, March 18, 1996, p. 12.

9. Steven Mufson, "China Nudges Brake Pedal," *New York Times*, March 6, 1996, p. 10.

10. Seth Faison, "Inflation Lower, China Cuts Interest Rates," *New York Times*, May 1, 1996, p. D5; and "A Fusion Ticket in Russia," *New York Times*, May 1, 1996, p. 18.

11. This is the theme of Evelyn Davidheiser in *The Paradox of Russian Politics: Economic Transformation under Tsars and Presidents* (forthcoming).